# The Unwanted Jew

## A Struggle for Acceptance

# The Unwanted Jew

## A Struggle for Acceptance

## Rosa M. Sacharin

DIADEM BOOKS

ISBN: 978-1-291-93930-9


Published by Diadem Books
For information, please contact:

Diadem Books
16 Lethen View
Tullibody
Scotland
FK10 2GE


www.diadembooks.com

This book is dedicated to my parents, who gave me life, and to all
those who suffered and perished during the Shoah.

The Lord is a refuge for the oppressed, a stronghold in times of trouble.

*—Psalm 9:9 (NIV)*

# TABLE OF CONTENTS

# Preface

I have now reached a ripe old age and it is time to look back in time. I will try to gather together the strands of my life and attempt to make some sense of all the events which helped, hindered, influenced and indeed made me the person I am.

My story is primarily for my children and the only grandchild I have. We all have a story to tell and some of mine is not easy. We all make judgments and are judged by others, but we try to make the best of any given situation—and so did I.

I am interested in history and particularly the history of the Jews, and throughout the years I have tried to piece together what I have been told about events of the time during which many of my forebears lived. Like many Jewish people, my family history is fragmented; records are no longer available and those who, perhaps, could have given information, are no longer alive.

I will try to piece together the events in my life—most of which are memories of personal experiences, others based on information I have gathered—and try to give a balanced view of the historical circumstances of those times. Much of my story is based on information my mother gave me and, I believe, is reasonably accurate.

Since my early life is centred in and around Berlin, it might be worthwhile to learn something about the city, in particular of the area where I was born. It was an area which played an important role in the political life of the city and where Jews, whether religious or secular, contributed to the social, political and intellectual spheres of life.

*Rosa M. Sacharin*

# Chapter 1

## Brief Outline of the Early History Of Berlin

The earliest evidence of the existence of Berlin is from the latter part of the 12th century. It was then the double town of Berlin and Coelln, situated on an island on the river Spree and a small portion of land on the north bank of the river facing the island.

By 1272 it had a Council which consisted mainly of traders. As elsewhere in the world, the Jews were primarily engaged in money lending or as lower ranking partisans. Berlin-Coelln went through a period of lawlessness with much robbery in evidence.

It was an independent Hanseatic city in the Middle Ages; though still small, it became the capital of the electors of Brandenburg from the 15th century onwards.

Berlin was founded by Germanic tribes, who migrated westward and was then followed by Slavs. These were subdued by Albert I the Bear, a Saxon who crossed the river Elbe from the west. His successors took the title of Margrave of the mark (border territory) of Brandenburg. Berlin still retains as its symbol a defiant black bear standing on its hind legs.

In 1411 the Mark of Brandenburg came under the governorship of the Nürnberg feudal baron Frederick VI, beginning Berlin's association with the Hohenzollerns, who from the end of the 15th century, as prince electors of Brandenburg, established Berlin-Coelln as their Capital and permanent residence.

It was during the reign of Frederick William the Great Elector in the 17th century that Berlin expanded and many new buildings, including fortifications, were erected. He also developed a canal network connecting Berlin to Breslau and Hamburg, gaining access to the sea. Since it was situated between east and west Europe it became an important commercial centre. As its sovereigns grew more significant in Europe from the middle 18th century, so did the city, achieving world importance after becoming the German imperial capital in 1871.

By 1920, the city had expanded and was unified under metropolitan administration to become Greater Berlin, and by 1939 the city's population had reached 4,300,000. The narrow streets and alleys of the medieval town became what was known as Berlin Mitte and the Scheunenviertel (so called because it contained the harvest stores). This area contained many substandard houses and slum dwellings, which were re-build in the 19th century and remained largely intact, until many of the houses were destroyed by massive bombing during the Second World War.

# Chapter 2

## The Jews in Berlin

Like Jews elsewhere in Europe, the Jewish population in Berlin must have originated from the Middle East country of Palestine, a name given by the Romans as a result of the defeat of Judah—thus removing the name Judea. The name Palestine is based on the early inhabitants, the Philistines. Following their expulsion from Palestine, Jews moved to many different lands setting up communities, using a variety of routes. Many travelled to and settled in areas such as the Rhineland, and moving further east following persecutions. Since many of the names of those Jews were of German origin one can assume that they had come from various parts of Germany, just as the Spanish sounding names meant that those Jews came from Spain. Delving deeper into the history of the Jews it is possible to learn how, why and when Jews arriving in various countries following the expulsion, changed their names to those of the population of the countries they lived in.

There is evidence that Jews settled in Berlin from the 13th to the 16th century. Most of the communities were destroyed as a result of anti-Jewish activities, as evidenced throughout the Christian world. One of these expulsions from the whole of Mark Brandenburg occurred in 1573. Many Jews fled to the east, to Poland and Russia.

During the reign of Frederick William I (1640-1688) many migrations of different peoples were encouraged, which helped to replenish the depleted population due to the many wars, limited food resources and resultant emigration. People came from the Netherlands and France (Huguenottes) and many of them were professionals, tradesmen or artisans. The Jews too were considered useful because of their experience in commerce. When the Jews were expelled from Vienna in 1670 and they asked for admission to Mark Brandenburg, they were allowed to enter on the understanding that they did not hold services in synagogues and only those with means or those with entrepreneurial capabilities were admitted. On the basis of these restrictions an Edict was issued and the first Austrian families received the letter of protection on the 10th September 1671. This date is taken as the foundation of the Berlin Jewish Community.

Despite the many restrictions imposed on the Jews, they were allowed to hold religious services in private homes and their children could have tuition from Jewish teachers. Legal representation in civil matters was under the jurisdiction of the Burgermaster of the town and criminal proceedings directly under the Sovereign.

Although the general population often complained about the Jews who were seen as competitors, the Jewish population grew and, by 1700, no less than 117 Jewish families were counted as members. Only 70 of those had the special Protection-Letters, but those made complaints against those who did not have them. There was obviously a rift between the two groups. The former felt threatened by the latter, who also had to pay extra taxes on their behalf.

Jews had limited control over their affairs. While Jews contributed in great measure to the general standard of life, every effort was made to keep their numbers and their influence strictly controlled. The poorest Jews were expelled. It was not until 1812 that Berlin Jews were given citizenship. Although they were not conscripted, many Jews volunteered to serve in the army. However, following the war the edict for citizenship was rescinded in 1822 as a result of social and political difficulties.

At the beginning of the 19th century, the Jewish population had grown to 3,000. By 1871 there were 36,000 Jews living in Berlin and by 1925 following the creation of Greater Berlin, there were almost 175,000 Jews.

Antisemitism has always been present in one form or another. During the emancipation, Jews were given equal rights, though some had more rights than others. While it was possible for Jews to be given German nationality, not all were encouraged or accepted.

Although my grandfather was given German nationality, his wife, my grandmother, was not given German nationality. At the height of one such anti-Jewish period during the late 19th century, many Berlin Jews were expelled, including my grandmother who was pregnant at that time (Bismarck period). However, when the situation improved, she was readmitted into Germany.

Jews were active in all areas of life during that period and contributed greatly to the German economy and academic life as well as taking an active part in politics. At the same time the Jews created their own organisations to support each other. In fact, the social organisation could be considered almost a state within a state. It had responsibility for welfare, education, health and training of young people.

There were hospitals, old peoples' homes, children's homes, schools and Institutes of Higher Learning. There were about 20 schools, a domestic science school and others, as well as a school for deaf and blind children. There were 12 Jewish Orphanages and Homes, five Old Age homes, one Hospital and one Psychiatric hospital.

By the 1930s there were 12 big synagogues and many smaller ones. Berlin was the centre where Reform Judaism was first established, but others also existed such as the orthodox, neo-orthodox, and liberal.

Members of the governing community were elected, consisting of business people, political groups, social organisations, and religious groups. At the head of the governing body was a Director who had overall control of all the different departments.

Political affiliations were also catered for within the Jewish community, be it part of the general political scene (except the National Socialist movement) or specific Jewish organisations such as the Bund and Zionist organisations.

Berlin Jewry was well endowed with newspapers and other publications. It was a vibrant and well-organised community, which played its part for the general good of the city and country and was efficient in providing essential services for the Jewish population.

**References:**

1. *Wegweiser durch das Jüdische Berlin*, by Nicola Galliner et al. *Juden in Berlin 1938-1945 Herausgegeben von Beate Meyer und Herman Simon.* © 2000 Centrum Judaicum: Berlin

2. *Gesellschaftskrise und Judenfeindschaft in Deutschland 1870-1945*, by Werner Jochmann (2nd Ed.1991). (Social Crisis and Hate against Jews in Germany 1870-1945).

3. *Verfolgung, Flucht, Rettung*: *Die Kindertransporte* 1938/1939 by Claudia Curio ©2006 Metropol Verlag.

# Chapter 3

## Family Background

The earliest memory of my life is from about 3 years of age. Therefore the early part of my life history is based on what I have been told in later years. I know very little about my father's early life and again I must use what little I know, from what I have been told by my mother.

My father's name was Israel Goldschal. I believe that he was born in Warsaw in 1897 and that he had two sisters. His father was a Rabbi. His parents were killed during one of the progroms. I had not been told the nature of the death of his parents nor the reason for the progrom. His two sisters emigrated to the USA but there does not seem to have been any contact between the siblings.

At one point in history Poland was divided between Russia, Prussia and Austria. The part of Poland, which included Warsaw, had at one time been part of Prussia but was later ceded to Russia. While under Prussian control, the Jews were encouraged to integrate into the then educational system. Many resisted that, particularly the very orthodox Jews. It was also during that period that Jews were "encouraged" to change their names to those similar to the general population.

While under Russian domination many progroms took place and there was a rebellion by rabbis. Many were killed, and the Jewish population was decimated. By the time the First World War broke out young Jewish boys were forced into the Russian army, including my father. Russia was part of the Western alliance fighting against Germany. These young boys were very badly treated and many were forcibly converted. My father, together with other Jewish boys, deserted and they were taken prisoner by the Germans and held in a prisoner of war camp. With the intervention of my grandfather (mother's father) he was released and settled in Berlin. In 1920 he married my mother. Post-war conditions were very difficult. Inflation was extremely high, with a loaf of bread costing one million marks. Homes were difficult to find and my father had little or no means.

Initially they set up home in my grandparents' home, which was a big flat in the district of Berlin Mitte. My father trained as a tailor, having obtained a Master certificate in design and tailoring. Both he and my mother worked together using one machine, gradually building up a sustaining and eventually successful business. By the middle 1920s the tailoring business had expanded and my father moved to business premises in Wedding, a district in Berlin. By the late 1920s he employed 20 workers, including home workers, and his clientelle included warehouses such as Wertheim and Hermann Tietz. His tailoring firm mass-produced ladies' coats, but he also produced coats for private clients.

As a young man he was very much influenced by political activists such as Rosa Luxemburg and Karl Liebknecht, both Socialist leaders who led the revolt in Berlin in 1918. As an employer he was meticulous in ensuring that the working conditions for his workers were good. Indeed, the laws governing employment were well advanced. When we visited his small factory premises it was always impressed on us how important his workers were and we had to go to each one of them, shake hands and curtsy, or bow (in the case of my brother).

I must have been quite strong-willed and was only interested in playing. He was at a loss how to "make me do his bidding", but would not let me play; after all, there were big scissors and lovely materials to "play" with. In exasperation he said to me, *"Roselschen, siehst Du die Arbeiter die so schwer arbeiten, es ist wegen deren Arbeit, dass Du Brot auf dem Tisch hast."* ("Roselchen, do you see the hardworking workers? It is because of them that you have bread on the table.") I turned to look at them and something must have clicked in that small brain of mine and I went to each one of them, made my curtsy and wished them a good day. It is interesting that

that event left an important impression on me and throughout my life I recognized and respected the dignity of labour of whatever type.

The premises were big with wide windows, providing good light and ample space for machines and staff. It had a small kitchen and a restroom. My father's office was well furnished with secretarial staff. As his financial position improved he felt a need to move out of the environment he lived in and establish his household in a more affluent area in Berlin. But this was never to be.

My mother's history was also eventful. Her name was Jochewed Jungermann. Her parents came from Prussian Poland and settled in Berlin in about 1860. Her father, Menachem Jungermann, was a Chazan (Cantor) as well as religious teacher and a businessman. His household and religious life were orthodox. As in many religious Jewish families, boys were encouraged to aim for some trade or skill or to become rabbis. The girls were not encouraged to educate themselves except to prepare themselves for marriage and motherhood. My grandmother's name was Blume Grosser. Her Father, my great grandfather, was a Talmudist in Warsaw. My grandmother was a big, dominant woman who, as was the practice, had many pregnancies. Not all survived.

In 1885, when antisemitism was very active in Prussia, Bismarck gave in to these groups, which consisted of well-educated people, and my grandmother, along with many others not considered full German, were expelled by the then Prussian government led by Bismarck. My grandfather had German nationality and could remain in Berlin.

My mother was born in Warsaw in 1897 and soon after, when the anti-Jewish actions decreased, the family returned to Berlin, settling in Berlin Mitte, where she went to school. They had a big flat in the Hirten Strasse and my grandparents earned their living by running a poultry and egg shop while my grandfather also acted as Chazan and led a small religious school in Berlin Mitte.

This part of Berlin was called the Scheunenviertel, and as already mentioned it was one of the oldest parts of Berlin and contained the harvest stores in its early history. By the late 19th century many of the buildings had been rebuilt and modernised. It became the area where Jews settled, particularly those coming from the east. It was here that orthodox Jews continued to follow their religious life. It was also an area with a great deal of poverty. People earned their living as small shopkeepers, market traders and travellers. Despite that, it was a vibrant community,the people helping each other and taking part in the wider Jewish and non-Jewish community.

My mother was one of twins. She had five brothers and two sisters. Two brothers became rabbis, the others were engaged in various trades. Two brothers were politically active and were imprisoned in Sachsenhausen Concentration Camp, which was in Oranienburg, near Berlin. One was released, the other escaped and managed to reach Palestine in 1934. My grandfather died in 1934, following a stroke, and my grandmother, who was obese, died of cardiac failure in 1936. My mother nursed both parents during their illness.

The eldest brother died due to natural causes. Her sister Mary married and moved to Poland in the 1930s and the youngest brother, Abraham, studied in Germany and became a rabbi. He went to Krakow as a rabbi in 1936 (see Brother's story). There is no trace of Mary and her family, nor of Abraham. However, my brother wrote about him and how he supported him during his sojourn in Krakow.

Erna, who was closest to my mother, married a shoemaker, a competent artisan but unfortunately, also a gambler. He died in 1932 suffering from tuberculosis. He left behind a widow with four sons and two daughters. The two eldest boys were sent to concentration camps and did not survive. Erna and her younger children included her daughter Paula, sons Sally and Harry; they were on the train to Riga, which they did not reach since they were gassed in the train which was to transport them to Riga. The only survivor of that family is Henriette (Jetty). She was sent to Denmark by Youth Aliyah and managed to survive by the kindness of the Danes. When the Germans invaded Denmark the Jews were to be transported to

Poland, but the Danish resistance managed to transport them, except those too old and frail, to Sweden.

Of my mother's brothers, who went to Palestine, only one was anything known about. Joseph and his family managed to leave Berlin in the early 1930s because the eldest son, Oskar, who was already in Palestine on Hachshara, was able to get visas for his family.

# Chapter 4

## My Own Family

As already mentioned in the previous chapter, my parents married in 1920. Following the war, housing was difficult to obtain and, as already mentioned, the couple lived in my grandparents' home. Indeed it seemed that my mother was reluctant to leave the parental home and this, no doubt, caused a great deal of problems. My grandmother was a very domineering person and instead of encouraging her daughter to set up her own home seemed satisfied with the situation. Of all the brothers and sisters, it was my mother who latterly nursed both parents during their last illness.

As a mother she was loving and caring but her relationship with her husband proved to be difficult. She took the commandment "Honour your father and mother" literally and perhaps had problems in adjusting to married life. In later years she told me that she had been in love with another man, but her parents wanted her to marry my father. This, no doubt, made her rebellious and affected her relationship with my father. There must also have been resentment. Not a good start to a married life.

My parents had three children. We were all born in Berlin. I will give a brief outline of Betty's and Brummel's life, since much of the details of my early life was similar to theirs.

### Betty Cilli

Betty was born in October 1921. She was always a shy child and certainly mothered me in my early years. As the eldest child she had the benefit of a warm and loving home, but later bore the brunt of disharmony. She must have suffered emotionally but to me, seemed able to cope and support us younger ones. The beginning of her schooldays was celebrated with the customary "Zuckertuete" and she started school in an orthodox Jewish school, called "Adath Israel". Later on she went to a state school in Potsdam and Hermsdorf. On returning to Berlin she went to the Ryke Strasse school, a mixed Jewish school.

Being old enough in 1936 when she was 15 years old, she was allowed to visit my father in prison and I remember this left her quite shattered. If I remember rightly, she became ill, with nephritis. She was quite withdrawn but was able to start work in a Kindergarten, which she always wanted to do. She had a good way with young children.

In 1939 she and my mother were threatened with expulsion. Betty managed to get a visa to enter Britain as a domestic, which was the usual condition of entry, but my mother failed to get a visa. I understand that the panic at the British Embassy or Consulate was awful with people desperate to get out of Germany. She left Berlin on the 1st September 1939 with one of the last aeroplanes to leave and arrived in Edinburgh to stay with me for a week until she was transferred to Peebles to work with evacuated nursery school children. Once the children returned to their homes Betty transferred to Glasgow. She was given employment in a Church of Scotland Nursery and was introduced to the Rev and Mrs MacDonald, who kindly invited her to their home. After the war she was able to take a course for Nursery School assistants, run by the then Glasgow Education Department. She successfully passed the examinations and gained employment with the then Glasgow Corporation Education Department's Nursery schools.

Betty married Henry Pheil (Pfeil originally) in 1949. He also came from Berlin in 1939 having been sponsored by the Misses MacDonald. Miss Lily MacDonald knew Henry's parents. As a language student she either stayed with Henry's parents or became friends with Henry's mother. Henry's mother was also a language teacher.

Henry's education was interrupted in Berlin due to the prohabitions of Jewish children attending State Schools. He had been a pupil at the Helmholtz Gymnasium and like other Jewish pupils was able to continue some schooling with ORT (a Jewish organisation—Organisation, Rehabilitation and Training) until he was able to join one of the Transports leaving Berlin. As mentioned, Miss L. MacDonald sponsord him and when he arrived in Glasgow in 1939 he obtained an apprenticeship with Weir's of Glasgow (an Engineering Firm). In 1940, when there was a danger of Britain being invaded by Germany, many enemy aliens over the age of 16 were interned. Henry was reported by one of his fellow workers for making an innocent remark, i.e. "in Germany we do things" etc. and that was enough. Despite the intervention of Lily MacDonald, Henry was interned and eventually sent to Canada along with a lot of Nazis, who were indeed a danger to the state. All the internees were placed in the same camp without taking into account the different categories. The Nazis immediately set up their own aggressive groups and it was some time before the commandant realised what was happening.

The Jewish internees were then separated from the Nazis. Henry was allowed to study there. Initially other Jewish internees, who were well educated, provided tuition and lectures which young ones like Henry attended and benefitted from. Eventually he was allowed to attend classes at a University in Canada.

Many of the internees were released when they volunteered to join the armed forces. Henry was very embittered and refused to do so, unless he received an apology for wrongful imprisonment. This was not forthcoming and Henry remained in Canada until the end of the war. On return he resumed his apprenticeship and qualified as an engineering draughtsman. His parents did not survive. They were sent to the Ghetto in Lodz (Poland) where, it is believed, they died in the nearby Concentration camp. Psychologically he was very disturbed and eventually required treatment. Henry died in 1984.

Betty and Henry had two children. Both were born in Glasgow. Maurice was born in 1954. Following his education in Glasgow (Shawlands Primary School and Shawlands Academy) he went to a sixth form college in England. He then started a course in Dentistry, but after one year decided to have a year out. He went to Israel where he stayed in a Kibbutz and eventually joined the Israeli Army. He met Marilynn, an American girl, and they married in Ohio in 1979. Although he had been in the Israeli army and was an Israeli citizen, he did not return to Israel. He eventually studied in America, obtaining his BSc and worked in chemistry. Marilynn and Maurice have three children—Anna Tamar, Sarah and Natan.

Rose was born in 1960. She was educated in Glasgow at Calderwood Lodge Primary School, the only Jewish School in Scotland. For her Secondary School education she went to Shawlands Academy and following her Highers entered Glasgow University. She obtained a second class honours in Languages (French and German). Rose married Leslie Smith in 1982 and they settled in Israel. They have two children - Ronit and Henoch. Ronit married and now has a son.

**Abraham Karl**

The second child was Abraham Karl (known always as Brummel). He was born in 1923. Being a boy he was much adored. As so often happens, particularly when a boy is born, my father took second place and much of the time and affection was transferred to him. Since I was not on the scene yet, much of what I surmised comes from my mother.

He was a typical boy and rather wild, at times getting into scrapes. He once got into a car and managed to start the engine. It was fortunate that the car moved very slowly and someone managed to stop the car before an accident could occur. Like Betty, he started his schooldays with the customary "Zuckertuete" and attended the Jewish school. Brummel and I were very close and while still very young, I often protected him when other boys attacked him. Indeed, when the boys saw me running to protect my brother they shouted: *"Hier kommt de Kleene"* (Berlin dialect) ("Here comes the little one!") and they ran away.

He did not have an easy life and much of it impinges on my life. As a result of much psychological trauma he developed a stammer and became very difficult to manage. He was sent to a special Jewish home/school in Marburg and gradually settled down. He was a nice boy with a good sense of humour.

In November 1938, when he was 15 years old he, along with many Jewish men, women and boys, was arrested and transported to Poland. I was not at home at the time but was told of the events and my mother's fight to have him released.

The arrests took place at 2 a.m. (when the body tends to be at a low ebb) and the event took everyone totally unprepared. After he was taken away, my mother ran after the van and went to the police station, but was unsuccessful in getting his release.

All of them were sent to the border in "No Man's Land". The Poles did not want them and the Germans prevented them returning into Germany. When they tried to run towards the German border, the Germans shot at them. They were tossed from side to side. Eventually he reached Warsaw.

Life in Poland was very difficult. He stayed in Warsaw with my father, but did not stay there for any length of time and went to Krakow.

I received letters from him in which he wrote that he was often hungry. I wrote to him about my life in Edinburgh and that there were apple trees in the garden and he wrote back that he had not eaten apples since leaving Berlin. I felt very helpless and did not know how to help him. However, I managed to send him a pitiful sum of 17/6 pence (saved from my earnings of 2/6 a week). He did mention that Uncle Abraham, who was a rabbi in Krakow, gave him support.

When the war started and the Germans invaded Poland, Jews in particular were singled out for slave labour and destruction. I did not hear from him and did not know what had happened to him.

I received one Red Cross Letter from him written in July 1942 in which he told me "that he had to work, but does not learn anything". He also mentioned that he was in touch with our mother and ended the short letter wishing Betty and myself all the best. This was the last news from him and since then I have not heard from him or about him.

I did not understand the purpose or meaning of that Red Cross letter and had to wait until 2004 when my search for answers gave me a better understanding. After the war I did make inquiries via the Red Cross about my father and brother but there is no trace of either of them. (See chapter on search efforts.)

I always felt that it would not be possible to find traces of all those who perished since the records available were mainly of those who were in organized labour camps, like Auschwitz, where each inmate was numbered. However, even there, their deaths were not recorded, while of those who were directly transported to the gas chambers or shot en masse, no records of those killed were kept.

*My brother – 1942*

## Rosa Mary

I am the youngest of my family and was born in 1925. Like my sister and brother I was born in the Grenadier Strasse, which was in Berlin Mitte. I was told that I was a little premature, but obviously not too premature. When I asked about my birth in later years I was told that I was not really wanted, but was nevertheless loved. It obviously was a time when my parents began to drift apart and I do not remember much about my early family life. I was a strong-willed child and not frightened to protect myself, or my brother in particular, since he seemed to be singled out for attacks. I attended the Jewish Kindergarten in the Auguststrasse and I remember Betty taking me there. I obviously was not keen to go and poor Betty had to deal with my outbursts of temper. I remember the play rooms and dining facilities as well as the rest room containing little camp beds. I also remember the adults who looked after us. We played, learned songs and had afternoon naps. I remember sucking my thumb to help me to sleep and this was not encouraged.

The year was 1928 and there was a great deal of political unrest. At that age I witnessed armed police on the streets. There were house searches and I remember our home being searched. I was too young to understand the reasons for it, but was told in later years that my parents and particularly my father was a socialist, much feared by the then Government. Certain songs were not allowed. I remember during one of these disturbances looking out of the window and singing one of these songs (*Brueder zur Sonne, zur Freiheit…*). My mother came into the room and stopped me from singing them, since they were not allowed. Some time later when there were frequent fights between the socialists/communists and the national socialists, a curfew was imposed on our area and I remember that we were not allowed to go out, or to open our windows. The police were standing armed with rifles along the street. I wanted to see what was going on outside and had opened the window. I heard a man shouting: "Shut that window or I shoot!" My mother rushed into the room to shut the window and said, "Do you want us to be shot?"

19

One day when the three of us were walking along the street, we were bundled into a car and driven away. I cannot remember who took us but we did not seem to be frightened. We were taken to a convent in the town called Küstrin. While there I remember crying and also remember my brother being very unhappy. He was beaten severely. Betty seemed to want to calm us but she too was very upset.

It was Christmas Eve; there was a Christmas tree and three chairs in front of the tree. We were seated on these chairs and I remember a man in clerical garb came and sprinkled water on our heads, i.e. we were baptised. Betty seemed to understand what was happening and told us not to tell our mother if or when she would come.

I cannot remember how long it was before she came, but as soon as I saw her I told her that the Pastor had sprinkled water on our heads. My mother became very angry and there must have been quite a scene, though I cannot remember much about it. I understand that there was also a court hearing and we were taken to a place of safety. My parents separated but did not divorce. Both were to have access to us.

In later years I was told the whole story. The relationship between my parents deteriorated. My father wanted to move out of the area to a more affluent one and also did not want us to be brought up in such an orthodox environment. Although he too came from an orthodox family, he was drifting away from the rather orthodox one. My mother was not willing or able to tear herself away from an environment in which she felt safe, and would not go with him. As time went on my father had developed a relationship with his secretary, Miss Hausdoerfer. Thus my home life was destroyed and for the rest of my young years, I, as well as Betty and Brummel, spent our days in Children's Homes.

# Chapter 5

## The Potsdam Years:
## 1928/9 - 1932

Betty and I were taken to a small Jewish children's home in Potsdam, while my brother went to the AHAVA, a more orthodox children's home in Berlin.

The earliest known mention of Potsdam is in 993 A.D., but it did not become a town until 1304. It was destroyed in the thirty-year war 1618-48. A new castle was built in 1660 and completed in 1670. It eventually became the seat of the Prussian Kings. It also became the "Military Town", with many well laid out estates and gardens.

Potsdam is almost surrounded by water and lies adjacent to Berlin.

The house we were taken to was a villa, which once, I was told, belonged to the Crown Prince. It was a lovely building with a wide sweeping staircase. It also had a very big room with lovely panelling and parquet flooring. We were allowed to use this room for special occasions and I remember playing "Ringe, Ringe Rose" with the other little ones. While I cannot remember our bedrooms, I can still visualise the dining room, which had small tables and sat four children at each. I do remember having problems eating and often was left alone to finish my meals. It was now a Jewish Children's Home run by Miss Recha Loewy (Tante Recha). It was not ran on religious lines, e.g. I do not remember Shabbat candles on the tables. One of the other pedagogues was Miss Anna Lohner (Tante Anna) who looked after the youngest children of whom I was one. There were only few children there of various ages. It was a loving home and we were well cared for. It gave us security.

While it belonged to the Jewish Community, our parents paid for our care. My mother and father visited us separately. In that way we maintained contact with both. My father, since he was financially well off, was responsible for paying for our care, which included our clothing and any other needs. Tante Anna later told me how much she learned from my father about politics and obviously was very much influenced by his views. It was that, amongst other events, which made it easy for her to work with Jews and remain loyal to them. Indeed, although she was a Catholic, she never imposed her religion on us children, but was meticulous in ensuring that we knew all about our religion. She took part in all our festivals, although I do not remember ever going to a synagogue while in Potsdam.

At bedtimes we were always tucked in with a good-night hug and kiss. When Bernard (one of the little boys) and I complained that we were so small, Tante Anna thought, to make us happy, she would "create a growing session". The kitchen in the villa was situated in the basement. It was very big with a big stove/oven. She, and others, placed baking bricks on the stove, recreating a yeast baking scene. Bernard and I were standing on these slightly warm bricks and, like dough, were given a teaspoon of butter and sugar. It was explained to us that these were necessary ingredients for yeast dough to rise and would therefore help us to grow. We took it very seriously and after a little while were wrapped in warm blankets and quickly taken back to our beds. We were very young at the time, 4 or 5 years old, and I remember the adults enjoying the session which Bernard and I were taking very seriously. We certainly hoped it would work, but both of us only grew slowly.

I remember two girls from Poland joining us. Indeed, they came with their mother while we were playing in the big room. While they stood watching us, I remember going over to the younger one and taking her to our ring play. We were told that the parents wanted their children to be educated in Germany. Krista, the younger one, who was my age, became my friend.

I had frequent attacks of tonsillitis and Tante Anna took me to the Berlin "Charitee" Hospital where the doctor advised not to remove the tonsils and that I would grow out of it. On the way back to Potsdam we passed the palace where President Hindenburg lived. Tante Anna explained to me who he was and I went to the policeman who guarded the gate. I said that I would like to see the President. He bent down to me and said, "You know, little one, the President is an old man and not very well." I said "What a pity!" and when I looked towards the building, the President stood at the window and I waved. I doubt that he saw me!

I started school in 1931 at the age of 6, the usual age for entering the school system. Potsdam, as I mentioned, had a military history and flavour and the first impression of school was seeing the older boys marching in formation in the school ground.

The first day at school was a tearful one for most of the children, but I do not remember crying, but feeling frightened. Although the other children had their "Zuckertueten", none of the "Heim" children had any. I do not remember being envious. It is interesting that both Betti and Brummel had Zuckertueten but because I was not at home, did not.

Although the school was co-educational, girls and boys did not share the same classroom. The teacher was called Miss Lehmann and she had a young assistant to help her with us newcomers. Miss Lehmann was a kind person and since I was small she called me "Primula". I already had a name of endearment, "Roeschen", which means Rosebud, and I was called by that name until I arrived in England. As far as I can remember, I coped well with school.

# Chapter 6

## Berlin-Hermsdorf 1932-1935

In 1932 the home in Potsdam was closed and we were all transferred to a smaller house in Berlin-Hermsdorf, which was part of greater Berlin. The distance from Berlin Mitte was about ten miles. The house was big enough to accommodate all the children from the Potsdam home. It had a large garden, at the end of which was a big shed that we used as a Sukkah. During the festival of Sukkoth we ate our meals in it. In fact, we decorated it in preparation for the festival with twigs and leaves gathered from the nearby forest.

Like Potsdam, it was a homely place. We were grouped according to age and Tante Anna was in charge of our group. We went to the local school, which was the 17th Volksschule. Like the school in Potsdam it was co-educational but girls and boys did not share the same classroom. Our form teacher was Mrs Schmidt, a delightful person. She was particularly loving towards us, the "Heimchildren". Arithmetic was my weak subject and she always made a point of giving any child who required it, extra tuition. I remember these sessions with fondness, for it was then that I not only began to understand the concepts of arithmetic, but also began to like it.

At Christmas time she gave each child in her class a gift, and her husband acted as Santa Claus.

In January 1933 Hitler became Chancellor and when President Hindenburg died in 1934 Hitler assumed complete power. We used to have many walks in the nearby forest and swam in the nearby Waldsee. The day that Hindenburg died we were walking in the forest and, as was usual, were singing, when a woman shouted to us: "Have some respect, President Hindenburg has died!" We immediately stopped singing and returned to the home. It was also to be the turning point for our relative peace. Indeed, when Hitler assumed power, every house was flying the new flag with the Swastika.

The changes were palpable from the beginning. We went to school as usual but school life had changed. We stood in the school playground and saw a stretcher brought out. It was the Janitor. It was rumoured that he had committed suicide. We had a new headmaster. He wore a black uniform, the uniform of the SS (Schutzstaffel, which became the Gestapo).

Each class stood regimented around the flagpole and the new flag of Germany (the Swastika), was hoisted. We were taught to salute the flag by raising our right arm in the Nazi salute and sang the National Anthem plus the song to salute the flag (*Die Fahne hoch*).

Following the ceremony we went to our classroom. Mrs Schmidt stood in front of the class and announced: "As long as I am your teacher here, no Jewish child will be insulted or hurt." That took a lot of courage since, early on, the children were encouraged to report anything that was "anti" Hitler in words or deeds. When Mrs Schmidt became pregnant and left, our world in the school changed for the worse.

The school day used to start with the "Lord's Prayer—All Father", but this was changed to "Heil Hitler"—and immediately followed by "Vater Unser" ("All Father"). In the children's minds it must have had the effect of equating Hitler with God.

Mrs Schmidt was replaced by a new teacher and changes in the classroom were immediate; Jewish children were marked out and ostracised.

The new teacher, a Mr Feißel, wore the black uniform of the SS. He made a point of singling out Jewish children, however trivial the event. One day he hit one of us with a jotter because her writing was not neat enough and shouted at her: "Get to Palestine, we don't want your kind here!" We told Tante Anna about the incident. She came to the school and spoke to the teacher about the upset he caused by

25

his attitude. His behaviour towards us improved. That too took courage. I should say that corporal punishment was not allowed in schools. Any misdemeanour was reported to the parents who were expected to deal with their children's bad behaviour. We had a little "black" book where the event was recorded and had to be signed by the parent, usually the father.

On another occasion, when we were having an evening lesson outdoor, one of the teachers taught us about the stars. She said: "See that big star in the sky, that is the 'Jew Star' that is responsible for all our problems." All the children turned towards the Jewish children and made suitably frightened noises.

The school week was from Monday to Saturday morning. Saturday morning was indoctrination time when children were introduced to the norms of the National Socialist State. Speeches by Hitler had to be discussed. This was primarily to be sure that the families listened to them. Children were also encouraged to report any comments made by their families and friends. Stories of heroism of Storm troopers and heroes like Horst Wessel were fed to us. All the children had to attend these classes including the Jewish children.

Another means of indoctrination was through the Youth movements. Girls joined the BDM (*Bund Deutscher Maedchen*) and boys joined the HJ (Hitler Youth). These groups were not open to Jewish children.

Anti-Jewish measures were introduced. For example, we were not allowed to go to the ice rinks. Arriving one day at the ice rink in Hermsdorf, there was a large notice which said: "Jews not allowed on the ice rink to skate." Tante Anna was with us and angrily plastered the notice with snowballs. When we wanted to swim in the nearby Waldsee, we were not allowed to swim there.

I enjoyed music. Our music teacher was an older man called Mr Lobel. We were given weekly music dictations, where we had to reproduce the exact notes and rhythms played to us. I was good at that. However, despite the fact or because I managed to write it correctly, I was always accused of cheating. A Jew could not possibly be good at anything. I was naturally very upset about it. One day when he came into the class and we stood to attention saluting the Führer, I raised my left arm instead of the right one. I was made to stand in front of the class, was duly harangued and made to salute correctly. Needless to say I did not like him. I drew a picture of him (not very complimentary) with the caption: 'This is Lobel!' I must say that I was not good at art. It must have fallen out of my satchel and one of the girls picked it up.

The year was 1935 and I was nearly ten years old. A law had been passed that Jewish children were no longer allowed to attend State or non-Jewish schools and we were to be transferred to Berlin. In fact, Goebbels made a speech in which he stated: "One cannot expect a German teacher to teach these Jewish children."

The last day at school, during the music lesson, the drawing was handed to the teacher. Needless to say he was furious, but since it was the last day I was saved retribution. I should add that corporal punishment was not allowed in schools but discipline was strictly enforced. I remember the smiling faces of my fellow pupils witnessing this furious outburst against me. It was really frightening.

My religious education took place in the home. There was no synagogue in the area, at least not near enough, nor did we travel to Berlin to take part in synagogue services. Rabbi Dr Klein taught us the rudiments of Hebrew and Bible. However, all the Jewish festivals were celebrated with much enjoyment. Purim was a time for dressing up, and Sukkoth was celebrated in the Sukkah which we helped to decorate. I remember how we collected twigs and leaves from the nearby forests and made the decorations. The meals were taken in the Sukkah. Chanukkah was also a special time when we were presented with gifts. In fact we were asked to write down our wishes. Needless to say the more expensive ones never materialised. I had wanted a violin but that was not to be.

My parents visited regularly but when we were old enough, Betty and I travelled to Berlin by train to visit our mother and father.

# Chapter 7

## Berlin 1935-1938

With the closure of the home in Hermsdorf we all moved to the Reichenheimsche Waisenhaus (Orphanage) in Berlin. This was the first Jewish Orphanage of the Berlin Jewish Community. It was opened in 1872 and accommodated 70 children. It was a magnificent building standing on a small hill in Weinbergsweg in Berlin Mitte. It had many facilities, including a gymnasium and large room with a stage where we gave performances at Purim and Chanukkah. Boys and girls lived in separate parts of the building, but during my time there, we shared our meals in a newly reconstructed dining room. We were divided into two groups each. The younger children were accommodated on the first floor and the older ones on the upper floor. We shared a dormitory, and played and did our homework in the large common room. Here each child had a small cupboard where we could keep our personal belongings and toys. The older children each had earphones and we could listen to the radio at nighttime. It was here that I first heard Shakespeare's *Hamlet* and *Romeo and Juliet* in German.

Tante Recha retired, but it was fortunate that Tante Anna came with us. This provided some element of continuity for us. The atmosphere in Reichenheim was very different from that of either Potsdam or Hermsdorf. It was much more institution-like, much bigger and had many more children. Indeed, as the situation deteriorated and more families broke up, more children had to be cared for in such institutions.

As in any institution, to maintain order, discipline had to be more pronounced. While we continued to call Tante Anna by that name, none of the other adults were addressed in that form. The head was Mr Oskar Friedmann, who had been a mathematics teacher and, I later found out, also a psychologist. While he was a strict disciplinarian, he was also kind. He was called "Director". His wife had the additional role of having overall control of the girls and housekeeping.

She was also quite gifted and was the guiding light in any plays and musicals we performed. While every effort was made to provide us with as homely an environment as possible, the very size of the home made it less intimate. Tante Anna, however, continued in her loving way and despite the many girls now in the dormitory, always gave us a good-night hug. We were allowed home every Sunday. Although I was not unhappy at the home, going back was not easy and I used to cry bitterly.

Children who were orphans, were taken out for the day by kind people. This was arranged by a committee, which ensured that all children had some contact with Jewish people outwith the home. Miss Stiebel was one of the organisers of this committee.

All the children attended Jewish schools, of which there were a great number. Betty went to a mixed school but I was sent to a girls' school in Auguststrasse.

It was quite a cultural shock. Although a well-run school and on the whole, well disciplined, there was a free spirit there to which I had to adjust. The girls were not inhibited, the way we were, but spoke out freely. Indeed, at times the classroom was quite noisy, which I found disturbing. It was interesting how the teachers dealt with these situations. There was no bullying, but persuasion. It often worked. On one occasion the class, an art class, was out of control, when the headmistress had to take over.

By 1935/36 many of the teachers began leaving Germany or were arrested. Their places were taken by less qualified teachers but who were experts in their fields. For example, our art teacher was an artist who no longer could function as such; our music teacher was a violinist, an older man, who no longer was allowed to play in an orchestra. We benefited from their expertise but they sometimes could not maintain discipline in the classroom. Indeed, the music teacher seemed at times to fall asleep and it was rumoured that his experience during his time in Dachau concentration camp had affected him badly.

Academically, the school was a challenge to me. The girls, who had started their schooling in that school, were far ahead in many subjects. In addition I had to learn Hebrew (modern) plus Biblical and Jewish history. Girls who came from a state school were given special lessons in order that they could later join in the classwork. Apart from all the usual subjects, we also had dressmaking and home economics.

Since it was a Jewish school the cookery lessons were held in kitchens, which were either for meat or milk cookery. We were also taught home economics and any meals prepared had to be costed. On the whole I coped well and although not a brilliant pupil, I had no difficulty with most subjects. I loved German as a language and its literature; I enjoyed History, Biblical, Jewish, German and World history as well as Geography. However, mathematics was not my strong subject.

In September 1935 the Nüremberg Laws were passed. These laws decreed who was an Aryan and who was not. It created restrictions on anyone not considered an Aryan. Jews were deprived of their citizenship and their livelihood. Contact between Jews and non-Jews either on a personal or business level was considered a crime. Mixed marriages were targeted and often led to forced break-ups.

A trial took place in which over 200 Jewish men were tried and found guilty of such contact and sentenced to periods of imprisonment ranging from six months to one and a half years. My father was one of them. All his civil rights were taken from him and his factory and belongings confiscated. I did not see him again. Betty was then 15 years old and was allowed to visit him once. She was badly shaken by that experience. In 1937 he was expelled and sent to Poland. Our financial situation became extremely difficult.

While we were relatively safe in the home, others suffered constant harassment. Homes were raided and arrests were made. Walking along the street became hazardous. One day a non-Jewish neighbour's child came to my mother and asked for help. The family was communist and was also persecuted by the Nazis. The father had been imprisoned in a Concentration camp and the mother's home was often raided. Their children were constantly harassed to join the Hitler Youth groups, but the parents resisted.

My mother took us to his home were we saw the distress of the mother and the destruction caused by the raiders who were the "Brownshirts", i.e. "S.A. men". My mother helped to tidy up and gave comfort and support. It gave me some first-hand experience of what the Nazis were capable of. It also heightened my anxiety. My mother was a very courageous person and a fighter. Indeed this helped her to survive in the terrible years to come.

Allegiance to the flag was demanded of all and since marches were often held, the people were expected to stand at the kerbside and salute the flag and the marchers. It was another way of intimidating the population and often created episodes of fights.

On one of these occasions when we were walking along the street, there was a march-past. My mother refused to stand and salute. We were very frightened and begged her to go into a house but she insisted that as a free human being no-one had the right to force her into behaviour which was against her wishes and beliefs. She was always ready to defend her home and conscience and had no hesitation in telling any Nazi what she thought of him and his regime. However, because we were very frightened she gave in to our pleas and hid in a nearby house until the marchers had passed. I am sure she realized that our behaviour might be dangerous not only for herself but also for us.

Children learn from their parents and other adults and I, too, in my own way, defended myself. Older children in their Nazi uniforms were used to collect funds for the Nazis. One day a boy in HJ uniform rang the bell and when my mother opened the door, he asked for money for the "Wintershilfe", i.e. for people in need during the winter months. I stood beside her when she told him in no uncertain terms: "I do not give a Pfennig to that Criminal!" The boy quickly ran away. I thought that was a bit dangerous and too outspoken and she was lucky that there was no attack on her.

Walking along the street, boys or girls would accost us and bar our way. Sometimes they would attack us. One day when Betty, Jetty and I were walking along the street, three boys barred our way and said: "Jews are not allowed to pass." Betty and Jetty ran away but I stood my ground and I slapped the face of one of them. It was such a surprise to them that they ran away. So did I. We were no longer able to go swimming or go on outings. Jews were not allowed to go into the Parks or sit on Park benches.

The 1$^{st}$ of May 1938 was the National Socialist Workers' Day and Hitler was to address the Nation at the Exerzierplatz in Berlin. Betty, Jetty and I decided to go and listen to the speech. My mother readily agreed that we should go but advised us to be careful.

When we arrived the assembled crowd and the army were in place when Hitler and his entourage, Goebbels, Goering, Himmler arrived, and the crowd greeted them enthusiastically. Hitler's speech was the usual diatribe with the usual accusations about the Jews, to the effect that they were responsible for all the ills facing Germany. He also threatened that should there be war, he would hold the Jews responsible and went on to say what he would do to them. The crowd clapped and "Sieg Heil-d" in full agreement with everything he said. Hitler's mode of speaking was the usual high-toned, almost hysterical form, which certainly helped to arouse the huge crowd there.

I did not feel frightened then and the people around us paid no attention to us. Once he finished his speech, and the National Anthem was sang, Hitler and his entourage left and the army was dismissed with due fanfare.

It was an impressive display of power and theatre, full of hatred. As people began to disperse we should have turned right to go home, but were pulled along by the crowd and reached the Reichskanzlei.

The square in front of the Reichskanzlei was full of women dressed in their finery and Dirndls. Their dialects were not one heard in Berlin, nor did adult Berlin women wear Dirndls. Little girls wore them and looked very pretty.

I thought they were Austrians or from South Germany, or even from Sudetenland. They were facing the balcony where they expected Hitler to appear. They kept shouting: "We want our Fuehrer!" When we arrived at the square the women gave us space in front of them so that we had an excellent view of the proceedings, which were to follow.

In time the balcony door opened and Hitler, Himmler and Goering appeared. The women went berserk, pushed forward to be closer to Hitler and since we were at the front we were pushed close to the balcony. They were hysterical, wanting to touch him, some of them weeping and totally out of control. While at first I was not frightened, this was terrifying. There stood big fat Goering dressed in uniform and covered with medals, smiling. Himmler grinned in his crooked way and Hitler smirked and the expression said it all: "I have got you where I want you, and I can do anything I want with you!" It was a very frightening experience to see and feel such evil power. We finally managed to extricate ourselves from the hysterical women and then ran home.

In the summer of 1938 we were on holiday in Agnetendorf, a village in the Riesengebirge, Sudetenland, where we stayed in a Jewish Boarding School, which was closed during the school holidays. We were sitting on the lawn and Mr Friedmann held a discussion with us when we heard singing in the distance. As the sound came closer we recognized children's voices singing and as they approached our group we became anxious. Mr Friedmann told us not to look at them when they reached us and to continue our discussion. As the large group reached us it consisted of uniformed

Hitler Youths whose voices sang loudly and clearly: "…and we shall rejoice when we see the blood of Jews (Judenblut) running down our streets…"

Mr Friedmann tried to calm us and it was very difficult to concentrate on what he was saying, but he managed to keep us calm enough and we remained seated on the lawn until the large group of boys, accompanied by their leader, passed. It was important that we did not panic, which could have led to an attack on us. We were a small group of children compared to the large group of Hitler Youths who passed by us.

## The situation worsens

In November 1938 my brother, together with many other Jews over 15 years of age, were expelled to Poland. I was not at home at the time. Much of what followed was what I had gleaned from my mother:

At 2 a.m. the police came to our flat in the Linienstrasse and took my brother away. The suddenness of the action took them by surprise. My mother tried to prevent the police taking him but was not successful. She dressed quickly and went to the nearest police station where many were held, but she was not able to rescue him.

Berlin is not far from the Polish border and they were quickly, virtually dumped on the border. They did not even have time to pack a case, nor take any food or money. Nor did the Poles want them. Poland had about three million Jews and anti-Semitism was rampant. (See Brummel's story.) When the Germans invaded Poland in 1939, the Jews were destined for destruction with the help of many Poles.

Among those expelled were the parents of Hershel Grynspan. Hershel was in Paris at the time staying with family. He was angry at the treatment of his parents. He bought a pistol and went to the German Embassy in Paris with the intention of shooting the Ambassador. He was led into the room of the first Secretary, Vom

Rath, and told him why he was there—and shot him. Vom Rath was not killed outright but died later that day. It is claimed that he was allowed to die to increase the impact of what was to follow. Indeed, it provided the Nazis with an excuse to unleash its destructive hatred of the Jews.

During the night of the 9th/10th November 1938, there was a well-organised attack on Jewish shops and homes. I was not aware of the riots and arson, since the Home was not attacked. It was only when I went to school that I became aware of the silence of the streets. Normally by 8 o'clock in the morning the streets were busy with people going to work and children going to school. That morning there seemed to be an eerie silence. It was only when I arrived at school that it became clear that something dreadful had happened.

There was a great deal of crying and some girls were beyond reasoning. Others threatened to throw themselves down the stairwell. The teachers had a very difficult time calming the children and preventing them harming themselves. Fathers had been arrested, some killed. Homes had been destroyed. We were all very frightened. Lessons were unthinkable and the decision was made to close the school until further notice. (Indeed, all the Jewish schools were to remain closed until the situation was calmer.)

We were told to leave the building two at a time, at two minutes' intervals and on no account to stop anywhere, and to run home quickly. I did stop at the Newsagent near the school to read the headlines on the posters. I felt a hand on my head and froze. A man's voice said: "This cannot go on, it must stop soon." I did not turn round, but ran home.

It was only later that I heard what had happened. That Jewish shops were looted and destroyed. People were beaten and killed; children's homes were set on fire. To crown the activities of the night, all the synagogues were set alight. The fire brigade was not allowed to extinguish the flames. There was one exception. The big synagogue in our area, called the New Synagogue, in the

Oranienburger Strasse, was saved from total destruction by the action of one policeman. He forced the fire brigade, at gunpoint, to extinguish the flames. To commemorate his action, a plaque is now in place on the wall of the reconstructed façade of the Synagogue.

The Ryke Strasse Synagogue was also not destroyed. The reason for that was the fact that it was part or adjacent to other buildings, which would have been damaged too.

The Reichenheimsche Orphanage, where I stayed, had not been attacked and we were not aware of the tumult of the night. There was a strong smell of burning but we did not know the reason. We were later told why we were left in peace. Beside the home was a police station. During the uprising in 1918 the Police station was attacked and the home provided shelter to the police. It was that action which ensured the safety of the home during the night of broken glass or "Kristallnacht".

There was further collective punishment for the Jews. A fine of one billion marks was imposed and all valuables were to be handed in. Germany was preparing for war and its coffers were empty. This was one way of paying for the war. All Jewish businesses were to be "aryanised" and minimal payment given for them. In addition, anyone emigrating had to pay a tax before they could leave.

# Chapter 8

## Preparation for Leaving Germany

There was panic among the Jews. It must be said that many Jews had already left Germany, particularly those who had means to support themselves in the country where they sought shelter. Fortunately, there were people with vision and great efforts were made to help us escape.

In Germany, Rabbi Dr Leo Baeck was an early advocate of organised emigration. He succeeded in persuading various religious, social and political groups to work together. He became a link between the German authorities and sympathisers overseas. He contacted Mr Otto Schiff, who had emigrated to Britain in the late $19^{th}$ century, and emphasized the urgency of the situation. Among the most actively involved were the British Jews who started collecting funds already in 1933 when the active persecution of Jews began in Germany. I learned about the generosity of British Jews when I was working in the Scottish Jewish Archives. These funds helped those of us who found refuge in Britain.

The Jewish orphanages and homes in Germany no longer could cope with the number of children requiring shelter and asked for help.

As already mentioned, the Jews in Britain had formed committees and were actively collecting money. When the situation deteriorated Rabbi Dr Leo Baeck contacted Mr Otto Schiff, who consulted with other committee members and approached the British Government seeking permission to allow children to enter Britain. There was some concern and opposition but eventually an agreement was reached. Although no figure was quoted, eventually over 9000 children between the ages of 4 and 17 were able to come. There were conditions of entry for the children, i.e. they must be unaccompanied, which meant no parents or relatives; also, they can be allowed in to receive education, but not allowed employment and, where possible, should be settled elsewhere as soon as possible. (Ref. *Men of Vision: Anglo-Jewry's Aid to Victims of the Nazi Regime*, by © 1998 Amy Zahl Gottlieb.)

By 1938, Hitler had annexed Austria and also had made inroads into the Sudetenland, and this created dreadful problems for Jews in those countries too. It was considered imperative to remove children from these countries as well as from Germany. It was hoped that children could be sponsored, but not enough people were willing or able to take on such a responsibility. Time was of the essence since it became clear that war was approaching fast. It also became increasingly clear that Hitler's dream of a *"Judenfrei Europe"* was becoming a reality.

A number of organisations already existed to help refugees—for example, the Children's Inter-Aid Committee, later to be called the Refugee Children's Movement. Money was collected and people were asked to sponsor children as well as adults. Not many Jewish families offered to sponsor children initially but eventually they did. Children from orthodox families were placed with orthodox families in Britain or hostels were opened for them. There were non-Jewish groups like the Society of Friends (Quakers) who brought children over, primarily those who were Christian or children of mixed marriages.

Many Jewish children were taken into non-Jewish homes or children's homes. Many were converted. The Christadelphians also played a part. They seemed to respect the children's religious beliefs.

Jewish Committees were formed in major cities to find suitable homes for children who came without parents. It had been the intention to inspect or vet the sponsors, but time did not allow for that, nor were there enough suitable people to undertake such a task.

At the end of November I was told that I would be leaving Germany for England. There was no time for elaborate preparations or packing. The transport was due to leave on the 1st December 1938. This was to be the first "Kindertransport". We did not require visas, as was the usual means of entry into any country of prospective immigrants. However, it was made clear that we should not be a burden to the taxpayer and no financial help would be available from the State. It was also hoped that the children would be able to emigrate to other countries. Many children and adults did so. The adults could only enter Britain as domestic workers, though well-qualified adults were sponsored by universities. Also, those who were financially able to make a living or were able to provide employment to British workers, were readily accepted but were directed where to set up their enterprises. This was to avoid competition with existing businesses.

*Last photograph with my mother before leaving Germany –*
*November 1938*

This document of identity is issued with the approval of His Majesty's Government in the United Kingdom to young persons to be admitted to the United Kingdom for educational purposes under the care of the Inter-Aid Committee for children.

**THIS DOCUMENT REQUIRES NO VISA.**

PERSONAL PARTICULARS.

Name *GOLDSCHAL, Rosa*

Sex *female*      Date of Birth *23.3.1925*

Place *Berlin*

Full Names and Address of Parents *— dead*

*orphan, Reichenheimsch Waisenhaus*

*Berlin*

PHOTOGRAPH

*43418*

*Copy of my document of identity minus photograph*

The quota system for most countries was carefully controlled, nor did the urgency of the situation cause any country to relax their restrictions. However, many countries placed even greater restrictions on Jews. A ship, called the *St Louis*, with Jewish refugees, some with entry visas on board and promise of entry to Cuba, could enter, while others were not allowed to disembark. Even when they neared Florida and sought admission, the US Government refused them entry. The captain of the ship reluctantly returned to Europe. Some of the refugees were admitted to Holland, Belgium and France as well as Britain. Many of those entering Holland, Belgium and France, did not survive.

Holland was one of the very few countries which allowed entry and short stay as well as providing means of transit.

The selection of children must have been a difficult task. The majority of children were Jewish and since they were members of the Jewish Communities in Germany and Austria, these were easily traced. Those who were classified as half or quarter Jewish, not being part of the Jewish Communities were helped by their church or non-Jewish organisations. It also included a small number of children who were non-Jewish, whose parents were usually political prisoners or under threat of arrest.

Preparations to receive the children had still not been completed when the first transport left. Two reception camps had been established for those children without relatives in Britain and those without sponsors.

The main camp was at Dovercourt Court Bay, a holiday camp built by Billy Butlin, and the other one, near Lowestoft, was called Pakefield, which became the overspill camp.

In some ways it was a question of where one lived and also who one knew. However, the children in the first group were chosen because many of them were in homes or considered to be in greatest risk at that time. Many were already orphaned, or their parents had been arrested, and there was no one left to look after them. Since many parents were arrested and children were left on their own, room had to be made for them and some of the children already in homes were placed on the first transport. I was considered to be one of these and was chosen to join the first transport. (I was later to learn the reasons for the children on the first Kindertransport.)

Refs: *Verfolgung, Flucht, Rettung: Die Kindertransporte 1938-1939 nach Grossbritanien* © 2006 by Claudia Curio.
*Men of Vision: Anglo Jewry's aid to Victims of the Nazi Regime 1933-1945* © 1998 by Amy Zahl Gottlieb.
*And the Policeman Smiled: 10,000 Children escape from Nazi Europe* © 1990 Central British Fund for World Jewish Relief and Barry Turner.


## Preparation for the Journey

There is very little that I can remember about the preparation for leaving Germany. I was not consulted until told that I would be leaving in two days' time. I went to school to tell my class teacher,

Dr Frank, that I was going to England. The only comment she made was: "Why You?" It was a question that still haunts me. I could not answer and there is still no real answer. She seemed very bitter that I was chosen and I was hurt. How can one answer such a question? I just stood there and shrugged my shoulders. I was well aware that people were desperate to get out. None of us had any control over events. I don't remember packing a case, nor did I have time to say goodbye to anyone, including my family, what was left of it.

I was wakened early on the day of departure on the 1st December 1938. Mr Friedmann took me to one of the main stations, which I believe, was Anhalter Bahnhof. There was a group of children waiting quietly. I did not see any relatives there, but then most of the children did not have any parents. Our names were called, but I did not hear my name and became quite anxious.

My mother arrived suddenly and quickly gave me a necklace with a locket. She was told that she should not be there at the station, but she would not be deterred. It was a very quick good-bye and probably because of the tension and the suddenness of my mother's appearance, there was no tearful reaction. Parents were also not allowed to see us off; perhaps the authorities thought that there would be tearful scenes. There were no tears.

Before I went to the platform Mr Friedmann gave me gentle advise how to approach the situation and said: "Roeschen, be friendly." Although good advice, I did not find it easy to follow. Life had taught me to be cautious of people and I had to know them well before I trusted them.

We entered the train. As the train moved off, the realization of what this meant overwhelmed me and I began to cry quietly. We travelled all day, stopping at various cities to pick up more children until, eventually, there were about 250 children of ages ranging from 4 to 17. There were some adults accompanying us but we did not see much of them. I believe they mainly looked after the little ones. However, when the train was nearing the Dutch border the adults came and we were then told that the custom police would be coming to search our belongings and that, "On no account must we protest or cry, if and when, they took anything from us!" We understood.

There was silence when the frontier police boarded the train and searched our cases. They took musical instruments or anything of value. We said nothing. Once they left the train and we were about to cross the border, all hell broke loose. The older boys opened the windows, spat on the last bit of German soil and thus gave vent to their pent-up feelings. I sat quietly and did not take part in that exuberant behaviour. In fact I was quite frightened and thought they should have waited until we had crossed the border to show their relief at seeing the last of Germany. It was to be quite some time before I cried again.

At the first station in Holland the train was met by a group of Dutch women who welcomed us and gave us some food. I must admit that I cannot remember what we were given or if I got any food or drink. We continued on our journey to Hook of Holland to board the ship, which was to take us to England. The adults accompanying us had to return to Germany.

# Chapter 9

## Journey and Arrival in England

We were allocated cabins in the L.N.E.R. steamer *Prague*, each holding four bunks. It was late at night when the ship left the dock and we went to sleep quickly.

The sea was obviously very choppy and we woke up feeling sick and very unhappy. We rang the bell but it was a long time before anyone came. In fact, we were told later on, that all the children were seasick and the poor stewardesses could not cope. We were tired and miserable when the ship landed at Harwich, early in the morning on the 2$^{nd}$ December.

I remember going down the gangway and being stopped to have my label checked. There were many reporters there, though I cannot remember speaking to anyone. We were asked to smile, but I could not.

*Photo: arriving at Harwich Port 2<sup>nd</sup> December 1938.*
*(I am the 2<sup>nd</sup> girl going down the gangway)*
*Photo: Thanks to Getty Images*

*First group of children assembling in the main hall of the holiday
camp at Dovercourt Bay
Photo: Thanks to B P K Photo Agency*

*A little girl from a party of children drawn mainly from Berlin
and Hamburg clutches her doll. Arriving in Harwich on
2 December, 1938, she was then taken to a holiday camp at
Dovercourt, near Harwich*
Photo: Wiener Library

*This photograph epitomizes my own feelings at that time*
*Photo: Thanks to the Wiener Library*

Once all the formalities were completed, we were taken by busses
to Dovercourt Holiday Camp. It was a large sprawling area with
many little huts. There were toilet blocks and a large dining room.
Since the camp was built for holidays and summer occupation, the
huts were not heated. As far as I can remember, I had one blanket to
cover me and it was so cold that it was difficult to sleep. I kept my
coat on to keep warm.

We must have been arranged in groups but I cannot remember who led our group. All the meals were taken in the big dining room, where we also had English lessons in the forenoon. The local people were kind and on one occasion we were taken to the cinema to see the Disney cartoon film, "Snow White and the Seven Dwarfs."

When it was Channukah time we also lit a Menorah. The older children put on a play, which highlighted life in the camp in a satirical way, e.g. there was a scene depicting a couple arriving with a chamber pot and if a child fitted on to that pot, then he/she would be considered suitable.

More transports were arriving with children from Germany and Austria and it was essential that the earlier arrivals should make room for others.

A most disturbing part of life in the camp was the fact that in order to place children, people were encouraged to select those they wanted. It became a "children's market".

During one lesson a man came up to me and I was asked to stand up. He asked: "Are you Jewish?" When I replied, "Yes," he said, "What a pity, otherwise I would have taken you." It was awful. It was not the fact that he asked my religion, but being carefully scrutinised, that made me feel unhappy.

The committee obviously had difficulty in finding placement for many of us. The younger, and often, more attractive children, were quickly taken, but the older ones were more difficult to place. It was suggested that I should go to Australia, Palestine or Ireland. I refused to go to any of these countries. I felt that if I went even further away, the chance of seeing my mother again was so much less. I was certainly not keen to repeat the rough sea journey.

I stayed at the camp for three weeks and it was then decided that a group of us were to go to Edinburgh. My knowledge of geography was quite good and Edinburgh seemed to me not too far away.

# Chapter 10

## Edinburgh Period: December 1938—March 1941

About fourteen of us left Dovercourt Holiday Camp early in the morning and travelled by train to Edinburgh. It was a long journey and we arrived in the evening. My first view of Edinburgh was very impressive with the castle being lit up.

We were met at the station by Rabbi Dr Daiches and members of the committee and fairly quickly taken to our new homes. The car I was travelling in seemed very big and chauffeur driven and I wondered what kind of home I was being taken to.

*Group of children arriving at Edinburgh Waverley Station.*
*December 1938*

We stopped at a block of flats and I was then taken to meet my foster parents. They were friendly and very welcoming. It was a small flat, had two bedrooms, a lounge/dining room, a small kitchen and a bathroom. There were three adults and a young girl there, who was about my age, and a cat. We had difficulty in communicating but their friendliness made it easy for me to accept the situation. Bedtime presented a problem since I had to share a bed with two people. I cried bitterly but they were understanding and the next night I slept on the sofa in the lounge. Unfortunately the cat also shared the sofa with me.

They were trying hard to make me feel at home and said that I would be going to school, just as their daughter. I developed itchy spots and could not understand why. I could not sleep at nights. Eventually it was diagnosed as flea bites. These must have come from the cat.

I cannot remember the sequence of events. At some point someone from the committee must have interviewed me and it was decided that there was not enough room for me at this family's home. I was told that I would be moved to another family.

I was taken to a family consisting of an elderly couple. They had a big terrace house, which had four bedrooms, a bathroom, sitting room, lounge, large kitchen, scullery and wash house. There were two further rooms in the attic. There was a garden, well laid-out with apple trees.

When I arrived I was told: "We really wanted an eighteen year old, but you will have to do!" I must admit I do not remember being told by the committee lady where my placement would be or my role there.

They were obviously disappointed with me and not very welcoming. We did not get on well from the moment I arrived. There was no warmth.

Since I was still of school-age, I had to attend school. The school they sent me to was James Clark Secondary School. Herta, who came from Vienna, was also enrolled in that school.

Coming from a more progressive type of schools we both were shattered by the poor standard of teaching and the boring lessons. Neither of us had experienced corporal punishment in our school systems and found it terrible how often and for, what seemed to us, very unimportant reasons, the children were punished.

We did not really learn anything there. No effort was made to teach us English. However, at examination time, the teacher who taught German at the school was asked to give us some work to do. He asked us to write an essay in German on any subject we chose. I had been interested in the Napoleonic period and Napoleon, so I wrote about that. Herta did not know what to write and refused to comply with the request. I felt that she should have made an effort but she refused. So I wrote her essay as well. Her mark was higher than mine.

Before we left the school we had to take part in lessons of domestic management, i.e. basically cleaning a house. Since there were no modern appliances, we used brush and shovel to clean the carpets. The house was very dusty. It certainly was not a good learning and teaching situation. I left the school and started my life as a maid at the house where I stayed, getting two shillings and sixpence a week.

Originally I was given a nice room but soon was moved to the attic, a more suitable room for a maid. I was expected to do light housework, but once a week a lady came to do the more heavy work. I helped with the shopping and also helped in the kitchen. I also washed clothing.

There was a washroom with an old type of washing machine. This was worked by hand and had a wringer to remove excess water. There was also an old hand turned 'mangle' for the sheets.

When the lady of the house became ill, I was expected to do the cooking. I could manage simple meals, but when it came to more elaborate cooking I had difficulties. My lack of cooking skill became evident when I was asked to make a chicken soup. The chicken arrived and I thought it was ready for the pot. I had never before cleaned a chicken or removed the inner organs! I therefore proceeded to place the chicken with all its inners inside the pot. I could not understand why there was so much fat floating on the top. Fortunately there was a young lady, who had married a Lithuanian doctor and who lived in the house came, and I asked her for help. I had to take the chicken out and she showed me how to prepare it properly. When the man of the house heard that I had been helped he refused to eat the soup or the chicken.

The relationship between them and myself was poor. There was seldom a kind word and only criticism. I was lonely, spoke little and became very withdrawn. I created my own little world. It was at that time that I started to write a diary. It was the only way I could relieve my inner feelings. I also started to write short stories. I made a point of writing in German because I did not want to forget the language. Unfortunately both these jotters have been lost during one of my many changes of abode while in Glasgow.

One day the older daughter, a married woman, took me shopping and said to me, "You German Jews deserved what was happening to you because you were not good Jews." I was very hurt. It was also a very stupid statement to make. As Jews and human beings they did not show much understanding of the basic tenants of Judaism, themselves. While many of German Jewry became assimilated, the majority still retained many of the rituals, though in a less orthodox form. However, they practiced a Judaism, which, to me, seemed more compassionate.

Another time, when I was walking with one of the granddaughters, (who was my age and for whom I was to be a chaperone), we met school friends of hers and I was introduced as "Bobbe's maid". Two members of that family did show me warmth

53

and I once stayed with one of them while the elderly couple went on holiday. The younger daughter too was friendly towards me.

During 1939 I had no further opportunity to learn English, but I was allowed to join the Library. I read avidly and initially, mainly schoolgirls' stories like *The Chalet School*. This helped me to learn English. The refugee committee also arranged get-togethers for the children and I also attended the Refugee Club, which was near to where I lived. Most of the people there were adults and I felt "out of it". I did not attend often. On one occasion I was invited to the home of a Scottish lady who wanted to hear of my experiences. It was a rather cold house and during all the time I was there, she did not even offer me a cup of tea.

The situation in Germany deteriorated. I received a photostatic letter from my mother informing me that she and Betty were warned to leave Germany or they would be imprisoned. I asked Mrs N. if she could help them or perhaps give me some advice who to contact. Her reply was: "I have got you—I cannot take in anyone else." While I appreciated the fact that they could not be expected to take anyone else, I had hoped to get some advice about who to contact who might be of help. At the same time my mother wrote to me that my name henceforth was to be spelt "Goldszal", since the Nazis considered "Goldschal" too German. I was hurt; though I changed the spelling of my name, I resented it. Somehow those photostatic letters reached London; that is to say, I cannot find them and therefore presume that they were sent to London. (I had never before heard that Jews were forced to change their names if they were too German, but recently I was given a book by Robin O'Neil called *The Rabka Four*. In it he describes a horrendous event, when the members of a family, who bore the same name as one of the Policemen, namely Rosenberg, were murdered simply because it was his name and a German one.)

Letters from my father and brother in Poland also worried me. They were having great difficulties. Originally my brother stayed with my father in Warsaw, but the relationship was probably not an easy one and my brother moved to Krakow, where my uncle

Abraham was. He was the youngest brother of my mother and was a Rabbi. My brother had no work and no food. I was devastated. By that time I had saved a little from the allowance I was given, namely two shillings and sixpence (2/6p) a week, so I sent him a postal cheque of 17/6p. That is all the money I had. I know that he received it. However, that was the only opportunity I had to send him something. I felt very helpless.

The threat of war was moving closer. My mother sent me a large 'Hamper' containing linen, silver candlesticks, silver cutlery and a silver coffee service. It also contained a pair of shoes belonging to my brother. The letter accompanying the Hamper implored me to keep my brother's shoes "safe and on no account to give them to anyone. They were his!" I locked the hamper and it was not opened again until some years later when Betty and I shared a room in Glasgow.

## Betty's Arrival

At the end of August I received a letter that Betty was arriving on the 1st September 1939. She was lucky to get a visa, but my mother did not. I understand the scramble for visas was dreadful; people were desperate to get out of Germany, Austria, Czechoslovakia and Poland.

Betty had not been well latterly and when I saw her on Waverley Station, Edinburgh, she looked ill, thin and pale. She was then seventeen and a half years old. She was allowed to stay with me for a few days.

War broke out on the 3rd September 1939 and many young children were evacuated. Betty was sent to Peebles to look after evacuated children. Although Betty's visa was for domestic service, like all the female adult ones, she never worked as a domestic since her arrival. She had already started some limited training in a Kindergarten in Berlin and that helped her.

She was allowed to visit me for the high holidays. During the meal Betty cried bitterly; she was very homesick and, like myself, very unhappy about my mother and the rest of the family. We no longer could communicate by mail and we were very worried. Mr N. showed no understanding and in a loud voice said to her: "What are you crying for, be glad that you are here!" While we recognised that we were fortunate, we were also very much aware of the mortal danger our family was in.

Betty returned to Peebles for a short while but once the young children returned home she was sent to Glasgow. While in Glasgow Betty stayed at a hostel and was introduced to the Rev MacDonald and his wife.

I remained in Edinburgh working as a domestic until I was nearly sixteen years old. There was little evidence of war, except one day on October 16th 1939 when a German plane flew very low over our house. I had no difficulty recognizing the plane and could not understand how it was possible that no British planes were intercepting or chasing it. There had not been air raid sirens and there was no anti-aircraft fire. I ran into the house quickly to tell the lady about the plane, but she did not believe me. There was nothing on the news—there must have been a News Blackout.

The Germans were interested in bombing the Forth Railway Bridge and were reconnoitring to do so at some point. (It was only in 1999 that I learned about the air raid on that day. The plane I saw had been damaged during the attack at Rosyth Naval base, and the pilot was returning to Germany, which he managed to do. Indeed there was quite a battle raging with British naval vessels being attacked.)

Edinburgh and its environs were declared "protected areas" and enemy aliens over the age of sixteen were not allowed to live there.

One day in 1941 Mrs MacD. visited me in Edinburgh. The lady of the house was not available and since I did not feel at home, I did not offer her tea. I had not met Mrs MacD. before, but she seemed to know about me (obviously from Betty). She asked me a lot of questions and suggested I should come to Glasgow too. She left before Mrs N. returned and I told her of the visit. She was annoyed with me for not offering Mrs MacD. a cup of tea, but I explained to her that I did not feel I had the right to entertain her, since it was not my home.

# CHAPTER 11

## Move to Glasgow in 1941

Soon after the visit by Mrs MacD, I moved to Glasgow. Initially, I stayed in a hostel in Hillhead Street. It actually was a Nursing agency run by a Miss Currie. She was kind and often had refugees staying there. I became a ward of the Glasgow Jewish Children's Refugee Committee and was placed in a hostel in Renfrew Street.

It was not a Jewish hostel and was run by a Miss N. There were a number of older refugee ladies and some younger ones. The youngest was Renate who was my age and went to Woodside Secondary School. The other young ones were Betty, Jutta, Inge and others whose names I cannot remember. The older ladies included the Misses Friedlaender (Lucie and Marta), Ilse Fuss, Miss Pinkus (who used to play the old and badly out of tune, piano); and Miss Hilde Goldwag and Miss Cecilie Schwarzschild. The cook was Miss Wittelshoefer, who used to be a teacher in my school in Berlin. On the whole I got on quite well with the others, though I had problems with Miss Wittelshoefer. In fact, I had a big row with her ending with us slapping each other. There were many tensions there. The older ladies were not prepared to pull their weight and it was left to the younger ones to clean the house and generally run errands. I was also told to set and light the coal fires, which I also had to do in Edinburgh. I never found that easy.

Miss N. was not very understanding of our problems and difficulties and often made anti-Semitic remarks. For example, during one of the big air-raids on Clydeside when Glasgow too was hit, she stormed into the sitting room where we sheltered and played Ludo. We were laughing. She thought that was dreadful and shouted at us: "Our people are being killed and you can sit there, play and laugh. Hitler is quite right what he is doing to the Jews!" We were naturally very upset. After all, we too were in danger and there was no sense weeping and wailing; one had no control over where the bombs were falling. Not many houses in this area had air-raid shelters and this house certainly did not have one.

On my 16th birthday I received a little notebook from Jutta, which became my new diary. I was also issued with an "Alien's Registration Book". As an alien I was subject to certain restrictions. For example, any time I moved to another address, I had to notify the police. I was subject to curfew, i.e. I had to be at home between 10 p.m. and 7 a.m. If I wanted to stay out later, then the police had to be notified. There were also restrictions as to the areas I could visit, since some areas were prohibited to aliens.

Since Betty and Jutta were working and earning money, they were able to have a certain degree of independence, though they were still not allowed to live on their own.

My social life consisted of going to the Refugee Club, which was in a house owned by A. E. Pickard, a wealthy man, who was also somewhat eccentric. This house stood in Sauchiehall Street, where now stands the Glasgow Dental Hospital. It had a small restaurant and also rooms for group activities. It was primarily for young refugees and the ethos was very left-wing. I was used to that type of political thinking, so found it easy to join in. The main group called itself "Freie Deutsche Jugend" but some Scottish people also of labour and communist leanings often visited. We were taken on outings to the countryside and encouraged to join in dramatic activities. There were also lectures and lively discussions. Contact with the Jewish Community was limited, although I did go to Habonim and Maccabi a few times.

The boys, trainees and those at school, lived in the Hostel in Hill Street. This house was donated by the Garnethill Synagogue Congregation and was under the control of the Refugee Children's Committee and the Synagogue. I went there for Seder once and for other meals celebrating the high holidays. Dr Cosgrove, the Ministeri of Garnethill Synagogue, invited the young ones, including myself, for Oneg Shabbat to his home.

Mrs MacD. took an interest in both Betty and myself and we visited her home frequently.  She suggested that I should go to school, primarily to learn English, so that I would have better opportunities in the future.  However, the Children's Committee thought otherwise.  When I arrived in Glasgow and reported to the Committee, I was interviewed by Mrs Mann, who was in charge of the Committee.  She seemed annoyed that I had left Edinburgh and advised me by saying, "I think you should go back working as a domestic—at least you have a bed to sleep in."  I was upset and said, "I do not want to do that, I want to learn something and work so that I can support myself."

I felt that I had done my share of domestic work and in some ways had paid my debt.  Domestic work solved a great deal of problems for them.  It provided accommodation, since it was a residential post and it also meant that the Committee would no longer have to pay for me. I must say that my response was frowned upon and even those adult refugees who worked or helped in that committee considered me rude and thankless.

I was fortunate in that Mrs MacD. supported my view.  Indeed, she was very helpful and played an increasingly active part in my life.  As a minister's wife she knew many people.  However, there was a price to be paid.  Ever since I moved to Glasgow she tried very hard to influence me and, in particular, to convert me to become a Christian.  Every visit to her resulted in sermons which emphasised the role of Christ in the life of Christians,  and that I too could benefit from this  belief.  At times the pressure became unbearable.  I was invited to church activities, encouraged to join the Church's girl guides and junior choir.  I found it difficult to refuse joining all these activities, and was very much aware that I was being sucked into the Christian fold.  It reached the point when I was almost obliged to acquiesce, simply because of the efforts she made and my feeling of gratitude for her help.  I spoke to her husband, who was the Minister of the Gaelic Church.  His advice was: "Keep your religion, you are part of the people of the Book."  It helped me to resist Mrs MacD.'s efforts to convert me.  I was never forgiven for that.  I think she felt that, because of her help, I should be grateful and show my gratitude by joining her faith. I thought that was a shocking reason.

One member of her congregation was a headmistress of a primary school in Springburn. She agreed to take me into the school. I started school, albeit a primary school on the 25th March 1941. It was not easy for a 16-year-old to join in classes with such young children; however, I recognised that here was an opportunity to educate myself and to become proficient in English.

By May 1941 I was ready to move on. The Headmistress took me to the Commercial College in an effort to enrol me. Since I did not have secondary schooling, I was rejected.

During the summer period I went to concerts and ballet. I enjoyed these activities very much and it also meant that I was introduced to culture, which up to now I had not experienced. My love for music was re-lit and I heard artists like Myra Hess, Hans Gal, Frederick Lamont. Many of these activities I undertook on my own. Betty and Jutta were friends and, being younger, I did not really feel part of that friendship. In fact, I had no friends and often felt very lonely. I was very frustrated and unhappy. My future seemed uncertain, and the committee were pressurising me to find work. They were not willing to support me anymore.

After long negotiations, it was decided that I could go to a Secondary School and I started in Albert Senior Secondary School in Sprigburn in December 1941. I was given six months in which to learn as much as possible and then to find work. I joined the 4th year class studying commercial subjects. It was considered that the German classes were not suitable for me and I was given private tuition by Miss Marks, also a refugee, who taught me German and German literature. I enjoyed these sessions. I made good progress in all subjects.

In March, 1942, I was told that the hostel was closing and that I would be moving into other premises. Betty and Jutta were allowed to find a room for themselves and were considered to be independent. There was difficulty in finding somewhere for me to live. One day I was called to a teacher, Mr L., who had been told of my predicament. He suggested I should meet a young couple, also refugees, and I could stay with them. I visited their home in Clarkston, and although it was a nice house, I did not feel comfortable at the thought of staying there. However, eventually I agreed but I only stayed there for a very short time and they and I agreed that it was not working out and I left.

I found a room in a flat in Allison Street, which I shared with Ilse Doktor. There was no bath in the flat. I developed flea bites, which was incorrectly diagnosed as Scabies and had to go to a special centre for treatment. Originally everything went well; I got on well with the other lodgers, but soon problems arose and I left. I went to stay in the Nurses' Club with Miss Currie. By that time I was getting tired of moving from place to place. I had difficulty in settling down and obviously had problems relating to other people. Added to that, I was moving on the day the examinations were due. I arrived late, very upset, and did not do very well. I was fortunate that the teachers understood my predicament.

A new headmaster came to the school. He suggested that I should stay on at school and sit my Highers. Again I had to explain to him that I was told to leave school and start work. Mr Roberts' wife was a Councillor with the Glasgow Corporation and she arranged a meeting between the Lord Provost and myself. On the 20th April, 1942, I met the Lord Provost. I had tea with him and he asked what I wanted to do. I had always wanted to teach and told him so. He then said, "You just continue at school and do not worry about anything. Concentrate on achieving your goal." There seemed to be no objection from the Committee and I was allowed to stay on.

I had moved so often and found it difficult to settle down anywhere. The Committee finally agreed that I should move in with Betty and Jutta. We found two rooms in a flat in Great Western Road, with use of kitchen and bathroom. Mrs MacD. helped us to get some second-hand furniture and we managed to create a nice little home. I worked hard at school, since I had to cover other subjects now in preparation for the Highers.

Through the good offices of the headmaster, I managed to get work during the school holidays. This was at a bookshop belonging to Baillie Uncles. Many of the books were Communist literature with a great deal of propaganda. Initially I was detailed to dust the books and that was boring, but I was soon allowed to sell books and also learned how to package books for dispatch and storage. I received my first pay of 27/6p. It felt good to have a certain degree of independence. I got on not too badly with the landlord and his wife, but that was to change soon.

On the 4th July, 1942, Betty became ill. She complained of severe pain in the kidney region. Jutta went on holiday and returned looking quite well, but was not feeling well. We called the doctor who diagnosed Pneumonia and she was admitted into the Hospital. Then Betty also was admitted to hospital. I visited both of them, but Jutta's condition worsened and she was eventually diagnosed as suffering from tuberculosis.

I was left alone in that flat with my landlord and his wife. He was a 'special constable' and used his position by coming into my room to intimidate me. I was very vulnerable and frightened but I managed to get him out before he could attack me. This created a very difficult situation and the end-result was that I was told to leave the flat.

I had to wait until Betty came home again so that we could look for other rooms. She had been in hospital for nine weeks. Jutta remained in hospital. Her progress, if any, was very slow. There was no effective treatment as yet for tuberculosis.

When Betty came out of hospital we looked for rooms which we eventually found in Belmont Street, off Great Western Road. We had two rooms in a terrace house which belonged to the Misses Ross, two elderly sisters. When we first visited the house we were asked our religion and, when we told them, they seemed surprised and said,

"Are there still Jews then?" It was a genuine question, there was no malice. When they were satisfied that we were decent (Mrs MacD. gave a reference) they made us very welcome. We were happy there.

Betty and I shared one room in the basement and Jutta had a room on the ground floor. We had a small kitchen to ourselves and also a toilet, though the bathroom was shared with the other lodgers. Once Jutta was discharged from hospital, she and Betty went out together and on occasions I too went to dances. I did not enjoy these. I was not sophisticated like them and rather young for my age. I tended to be a "wallflower" and had difficulty forming relationships. I did not have "dates" and felt very much like a "fifth wheel on the wagon".

In 1942 I received a Red Cross Letter from my brother. It was a terse note of about 25 words (all that was permitted at that time). In it he stated that "I must work but do not learn anything". I obviously realised what that meant and I wrote in my diary: "I believe that he is in a labour camp and must work as a prisoner." I felt very helpless. At that time little was known about the conditions that our people were living under and the dangers facing them. It was only after the war that the full picture emerged.

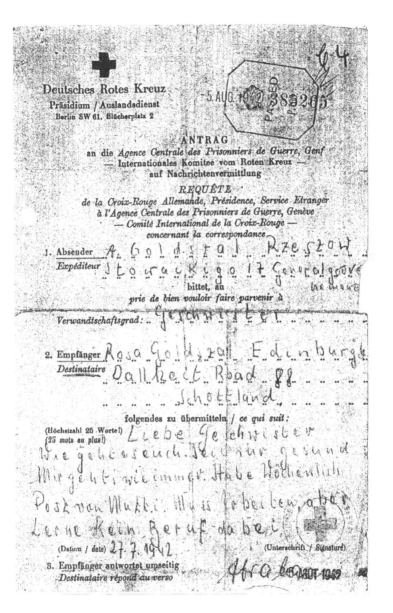

*German Red Cross letter from my brother*

In March 1943 we received two letters from my mother in which she informed us that Jetty's mother and her youngest sister, Paula, had been transported to Poland. She did not mention much about herself and were very surprised that the letter reached us. Jutta, too, received news from her father that her mother had died. She took it very bravely. She was not to know what really happened and also that her father would not survive his ordeals.

There were several air attacks, particularly in Clydebank, which was severely damaged. Many people were killed. Although the air raid sirens sounded in Glasgow and we heard the anti-aircraft guns firing at that time, most of the bombs fell on Clydebank. Betty had to do fire-watching at the nursery where she worked, and on occasions, when she did not feel well, I stood in for her. We also offered our help in a canteen to serve food to servicemen and women.

I was encouraged to join the Rangers, the senior branch of the Girl Guide Movement. This group met in St Columba Gaelic Church whose minister was the Rev MacD. I also joined the junior choir there. I quite enjoyed the choir. I was somehow drawn deeper into church life but still struggled to retain my Jewishness. During that period I had no contact with the Jewish community.

I sat my Highers in April 1943, though the results did not arrive until June. I now had to decide what to do. At that time, as part of the war effort, people were directed into war work. This also included refugees. The options for me were, A.T.S. (Auxiliary Territorial Service – Women), munitions factory, or nursing. I was not keen to do any of these.

In April 1943 Mrs MacD. suggested to me that I should consider going into nursing. I was not keen. I had no experience of hospital life and did not think that I would either like it or cope with it. There were obvious advantages to train as a nurse, but I was not willing to recognise or consider them. However, Mrs MacD. must have spoken to the Matron of the Royal Hospital for Sick Children at Yorkhill and in May I received application papers. With them I received information about uniform, etc. The cost was about £30, which I did not have. I resisted filling in the form and as usual was reluctant to consider anything at all. It almost seemed as if I was frightened to enter into any work commitment.

After further discussion with Mrs MacD., I was persuaded that the nursing option was really the best one for me. I would receive training, have somewhere to live and receive an allowance. It was an opportunity to achieve a degree of independence. I duly filled in the papers and send them to the Matron.

I received my results of the Highers examinations and was very happy that I had passed. I was also told that I would be getting prizes in English, Geography and Commercial Subjects. I was most surprised but also felt that I had achieved something at last. Prize giving was on the 30th June, when I also received the Higher Leaving Certificate. I was now ready to start a new phase in my life.

# Chapter 12

## Start of my Career

I was invited for an interview at Yorkhill. I was apprehensive and had a rather negative attitude. Miss Clarkson, the Matron, was charming and made me feel at ease. Despite that, I told her I was not very happy about starting the course. She obviously had been briefed already and was aware of my reluctance to start the nursing course. I asked her: "How long would I have to stay before I had to make a final decision?" She replied: "Well, Miss Goldszal, if you do not like us, or we feel that you are not suitable, then you could leave after three months!" I was also given a medical examination.

Two weeks after the interview I received a letter from Miss Clarkson that I was accepted for training and she hoped I would be happy in my training. Instead of feeling relieved at the opportunity, I cried!

On the 3rd August 1943 I started my training as a Sick Children's Nurse. The course was to last three years. There were five of us in that intake. From the beginning I became friendly with Vivienne. However, she too was not too keen to start the training so we tended to reinforce our antipathy towards the course and nursing in general.

Miss Sorry, our tutor, initiated us into the rudiments of nursing. She was a kind person and did her best to make us feel at ease. It was strange wearing a uniform with a frilly hat, which took some time to prepare and then to set it securely onto my head. I felt ridiculous in it and rather self-conscious.

We spent the first week in the classroom, but from 5 p.m. until 8.30 p.m. we were working in the wards. Here, we were taught the essentials, such as taking the pulse, measuring body temperature, making of hospital beds and cots and the giving of bedpans. Our introduction to nursing was given to us by Miss Clarkson, who stressed that nursing and hospital regimes were like the army. The senior staff representing officers; staff nurses, non-commissioned officers; and the probationers, the privates. It was also stressed that our behaviour towards the different grades must be reflected in due respect and deference towards them. Senior nurses should not fraternise with junior nurses. The day finished with prayers at 9 p.m. We were all expected to take part. A senior nurse stood at the door to ensure that all went down to one of the rooms, which served as a recreation room. Early on I decided that this was wrong, at least for me, and when I refused to join the prayer meetings, others soon followed.

After the first week we were allocated to a ward. I was sent to ward 9, a surgical ward. The ward sister, Miss Bone, ran the ward with military precision. As the most junior nurse, called probationer, I was expected to perform the most menial tasks. However, I accepted that and tried hard to work competently. The workload was heavy and as junior nurse was expected to carry out specific tasks within quite tight time schedules. The orthopaedic clinic was held on a Monday morning. We were expected to remove heavy plaster casts in readiness for the children's examinations by the Surgeon. It was very hard work and not without an element of danger, in that it was easy to nick or cut the child's skin. Since this clinic lasted all morning, the routine work could not be carried out. One of the daily routines for the junior nurse was to fine-tooth-comb all the children's hair, looking for nits and lice, and if found, to treat them. If that task had not been carried out, then I had to remain on duty to do so. Considering that I came on duty at 7 a.m. and if one had an evening off, either at 5 p.m. or 6 p.m., it was not unreasonable to expect to go off duty at those times.

I did not take kindly to being kept on duty. It seemed very unfair to me and I was really very tired by then. I eventually rebelled against it and while my behaviour was frowned upon, no repercussions occurred. I at least had made my point. After two months I was detailed to go on night duty. The ward was full of very ill children. We nursed a variety of conditions from accidents, burns, scalds, abscesses and post-operative cases of appendectomies, hernia etc.

During my first spell of night duty we had very severe burns in the ward. The suffering of the children, their cries and moans, as well as the smell of burnt and infected wounds, remains with me still. I was very frightened and became very anxious. There was no one to talk to, no one to help me work through the terror I felt. And it *was* a feeling of terror! Since there were no porters on duty during the night, when a child died, nurses had to take the body down to the ducts. It was very frightening for me and my imagination was also at overdrive, which increased my anxiety. In fact one of the comments made early on in my training was: "You did not come here either to be sick, nursed or comforted, you are here to nurse and comfort the children." We therefore never complained.

We were also expected to give a report to night sister when she came to visit the ward. We had to know every child's name, age, condition, treatment and response to treatment. It was a tall order. The first time I was detailed to accompany the night sister and report to her, my mind went blank. We went silently round about half the ward, when the sister stopped and asked: "Will you not tell me about the patients, nurse?" In my fear of the situation I said nothing but she kindly helped me and I was then able to tell her about the remaining children in the ward.

I became very much aware of the poverty of these poor children. Fathers were in the forces and mothers, on their own, often could not cope. Children looked neglected, undernourished and often very dirty. Their suffering was pitiful to behold and affected me very much. At that stage I was not aware of the home conditions, nor of the difficult lives these people led.

Vivienne still talked of leaving and I also intended to do so. However, I became ill with tonsillitis and was confined to sick bay, while Vivienne resigned and left. I had become quite fond of Vivienne. She invited me to her home and I got to know her parents. Her father seemed to me to admire Hitler and what he had done for

Germany. The sufferings he caused seemed to him of less importance. I was always welcome in their home and even though Vivienne left, I still kept in contact with her. (In my final year, Vivienne, her sister and I cycled from Bearsden, her home, to Rowadennan at the foot of Ben Lomond. We climbed the mountain and managed to get back down in time to catch the boat to take us back to Balloch. We cycled back to Bearsden and I managed to get the bus back to Old Dumbarton Road, arriving at Yorkhill with a few minutes to spare before my late pass expired at 11 p.m.)

Although in many ways I found satisfaction in my work, I was still not reconciled to continuing with my training. I also had difficulties studying and failed the first preliminary exams of anatomy/physiology. I spoke to Mrs MacD. about resigning and although she thought it was a mistake, she did not pressurise me to continue. I went to Miss Clarkson and handed in my letter of resignation. She spoke to me kindly and suggested that perhaps removing me from the stresses of the acute wards to a less stressful environment might be helpful. She felt that I should continue and would not accept my resignation. She was a wise woman and I was to be grateful to her subsequently.

In January, 1944, I moved to the Country Branch in Drumchapel. This was part of Yorkhill. Here, the children were either chronically ill or at the convalescing stage. It was less stressful. It was also a more relaxed place. One senior nurse, in particular, had such an easy approach to life and such an infectious laughter, that I too was affected by it. It also gave me time to think about my future and I began to realise how stupid my attitude was. I recognised the value of the training and began to see a brighter professional future. I began to grow up. I stayed there until the end of May. During that time I began to assert myself and, being of a rebellious nature, began to question attitudes and procedures—in particular the behaviour of nurses towards one another. The need for nurses to stress their status i.e. of seniority, however limited in time, resulted in many episodes of unfairness and increased tension between staff. My own view was that newcomers should be helped, not bullied into submission, which was considered essential for discipline. I did not share that view. At first that was resented, but with discussions, my colleagues began to accept my approach and by extension, accepted me. My work improved and I became surer of myself.

I did not look forward to returning to Yorkhill but realised that I must face that too and continue in the way I was developing. I returned to Yorkhill at the beginning of June. I re-sat the failed exam and passed it. I also made friends more easily. In particular, Irene and I became friends. I often was invited to her home and her parents were particularly kind and hospitable. Irene also came to our lodgings. We had many interests in common, in particular music, and attended concerts together. Later on we formed a music club in Yorkhill where we played records, which we all brought from home. My relationship with senior members of staff also improved. Miss Clarkson was always helpful towards me and when we asked to be allowed to have tea during our music sessions, she readily agreed.

To begin with I had difficulty with the theoretical part of the training but once I adjusted mentally to my profession, I had no problems and achieved good grades in my examinations. Anatomy and Physiology was taught by Dr Suttie, the medical superintendent, while the medical and surgical subjects were taught by senior doctors. All nursing lectures were given by the Tutor. There were no discussions during any sessions and basically one wrote down what was said and memorised it. There were very few nursing books available. Cath MacD., Mrs MacD's daughter-in-law, gave me a nurses' textbook as a present when I started training. This was the only one on the market and was a general textbook for nurses. There were no specific books on sick children's nursing. The study of psychology or child development did not exist. In the wards too, we carried out procedures as they were taught and no one questioned what was taught.

The syllabus was laid down by the General Nursing Council, which also assessed the hospitals for training suitability. While the hospital set its own examination, the intermediate and Final State Examination were the responsibility of the General Nursing Council. This was a statutory body, which regulated the Nursing profession and maintained the Register. Lectures had to be attended whether we were on or off duty and following night duty, after working a twelve-hour shift. It was difficult to keep awake then and take notes.

Children sat or lay in their beds and any untidiness was frowned upon. As a senior nurse, I took those children, who were well enough, out of bed. I let the toddlers crawl on the floor – unheard of! When Miss Clarkson came on her rounds, I thought she would reprimand me but instead, recognised my initiative. Every nurse, irrespective of level of training, was expected to know the name, age, diagnosis and the current state of the children. Since the wards held up to 30 children, this was quite a task.

Most of the senior nursing staff were approachable, though there were some who made life very difficult. Although no one openly mentioned the fact that I was a foreigner, some veiled comments were made. I took it in my stride. By the time I reached my final year I had become much more confident and was able to take responsibility at ward level. Third year nurses acted as staff nurses, since there was a dearth of this level of nurse. This meant that the senior nurse often acted not only as a staff nurse but also, in the absence of sister, at that level.

Like all nurses I gained experience in a wide range of wards and conditions. I enjoyed theatre work and spent some time in the accident and emergency unit, although at that time it was called simply "admission hall". Part of the unit was also the x-ray department. In those days it consisted of one room with an old x-ray machine, which was operated by a senior nurse. The medical Superintendent acted as radiologist. Sister Isobel was very old, or so she seemed to me. She knew how to turn the knobs. When I asked her how the machine worked, she replied: "Nurse, all you need to do is dust, dust, dust." So I dusted. In fact, we were not encouraged to ask questions and I always felt that even if I were to ask questions, the senior staff would not be able to answer them. In many ways I felt very frustrated and had a need to learn more and to understand better.

By 1945 the war was nearing its end. Germany was heavily bombed and the Russian army was rapidly advancing towards Germany. The Germans were still able to bombard London and other areas, but this was mainly achieved by rockets. The Battle of Britain had established British superiority in the air. The allied forces were successful in invading mainland Europe and although progress was slow, at least the outcome was more promising for the allies. I had not heard from my mother, father and brother since the last Red Cross Letter in 1942, but the news from Poland and any of the parts liberated indicated that not many would survive the ordeal. It was only when the concentration camps were entered that the full horror of what had been perpetrated by the Germans and their collaborators, became clear.


**Uncertainties after the War**

The war in Europe ended on the 5th May 1945. We were allowed into Britain on the understanding that we would return to the countries we came from once it was possible to do so. The destruction caused by the war made this very difficult, if not impossible. No one had anticipated the turmoil that now existed. We had nowhere to go. There was a constant movement of people who had been displaced by the Germans, either as prisoners or as slave labourers. Many of them were held in Displaced Persons camps until their identities had been established and a final destination for them agreed on.

Demobilisation meant that those soldiers returning from the different forces had to be given work and we, as refugees, would have to make room for them. In fact, Betty was made redundant. In some ways my position was less threatened because nursing was labour intensive and there was always a shortage of nurses. Nevertheless I was apprehensive about the future. I thought perhaps that I might return to Germany and help our Jewish people who had suffered so much. Palestine was another option, but the situation there was uncertain and the politics of the day certainly did not encourage Jews to enter. I was quite confused about the situation here and felt again very insecure. I had no idea what it was like in Germany but thought that it might be easier there than here. I was soon to be enlightened and realised that there was no future there for me.

Some of the refugees emigrated to America, but only if they had family there who could act as guarantors or had visas. We did not have anybody there. Questions were asked in Parliament about us, the refugees regarding our return to the countries we came from. It was Winston Churchill, the Prime Minister, who replied to these questions that "there was nothing for the refugees to return to". Eventually the Government offered us British nationality, but this took some time to be achieved.

I became very interested in Freudian psychology. I always felt that the nursing course lacked something and when I read a book on psychology, I thought that was an aspect of human behaviour I would like to know more about. There was to be a conference on Psychology and it was based on the work of the Davidson Clinic in Edinburgh. It lasted for one week. Mrs MacD. suggested that this might be of interest to me and on the 1st of August I travelled with her to Edinburgh.

On the first evening we had two lectures on "Psychology and Religion". The main programme started on the second of August and again the emphasis was to make us aware of the relationship between the soul and the spiritual dimensions. This was a new approach for me. Indeed I found it difficult to understand the language of psychology. While I found the atmosphere stimulating, it was also very frustrating for me not to follow the ideas presented. The majority of delegates present seemed to find it easy to take part in discussions and obviously found these sessions helpful. This was a new world to me and I realised I had a great deal to learn.

We were shown round the Davidson clinic and the work was explained to us. The method of treatment was by psycho-analysis. Children and adults were treated there. It was recognised that where children had problems, these emanated from the home and it was essential that not only the children were treated, but the parents too. I became aware that this aspect of treatment for anxiety and depression could help me in my work. It was also suggested to me, to understand the problems of the children it was necessary to understand myself, my own thought processes and attitudes. To achieve this, I should undergo psycho-analysis and in due course I attended sessions with Dr Rushforth, the director of the Davidson Clinic.

I found the experience quite disturbing but it also helped me to understand myself a little better. As time went on I was able to use what I had learned, to a limited extent. There were children whose diagnosis was difficult to make and I realised that other factors than bacteria or viruses could be at play. I remember one little girl, about one and half years old, who had persistent diarrhoea. No organisms were identified and all tests proved to be negative.

I observed her and thought she was unhappy, never cried and never called for her mother. However, she did call for her father. She never played and just sat. I decided to pay more attention to her, feeding her and whenever possible, playing with her. She gradually began to trust me and respond to me. The diarrhoea ceased. When it was time for her to go home, I took her to her mother but she refused to go to her. Her mother was very upset and accused me of "stealing" her child's love. Eventually she accepted her mother and went home.

I saw this child again when I was on duty in the out-patient department. I scarcely recognised her. I was very upset the way the mother handled the child and how frightened the little girl was. At that time, abuse of children was not recognised, but here was no love for that little girl. It made me realise how important emotional care was and also how careful I had to be not to get too deeply involved, since the children do go back to their own homes and any close relationship with children can also be disturbing for them. It is obviously also resented by the family.

# Chapter 13

## Contact with my Mother

In November 1945 I received a letter from a British soldier and soon after, from an American soldier. Each of them wrote that while at a Jewish religious service in Berlin, my mother approached them. She had remembered my Edinburgh address and they wrote to me. They mentioned that her state of health was poor and that she was lacking food. They offered to forward any food parcels to her. We immediately sent parcels to her. A short time later, my mother wrote to us and explained her situation to us, stating that she did not wish to remain in Germany. We still did not understand how terrible it had been for her and still was. We felt that she would not settle in here and perhaps we should go back to Germany.

Eventually we applied for her entry to Britain and had to write to the British Commander of the British sector in Berlin. We also had to give an undertaking to guarantee for her. Both our earnings were very low, but we felt we somehow had to manage. We also had to give some thought where we could live when she came. This was quite a problem.

The condition of her entry was that she would not be a burden on taxpayers and at the same time that she would not take employment. We were worried that we would not be able to support her. I also wrote via the Red Cross to Poland to ascertain the whereabouts of my father and brother. When I mentioned Rszezow, the reply indicated that such a place did not exist. At that time Russia was in control of Poland and I thought that they obstructed any news coming out of Poland.

I was now in my third year of training. I gained further experience in various wards, theatre and outpatient department. As a senior nurse I had more responsibility and coped well. I was still highly critical of nursing, both of the organisation as well as the practice. My relationship with the doctors was quite good, though on one occasion I had serious problems when ordered to give a child sedation simply to quieten him. This was not part of necessary treatment but to calm the doctor's frayed nerves following a night of drinking. I refused to carry out his instruction and was reported to the Matron and the Medical Superintendent. When both our sides were heard, he was cautioned and I was sent to West Graham Street, the out-patient department, as a staff nurse, after I sat and passed my Final State Examinations.

After the failure in passing the first Preliminary examination I had no further difficulties and, in fact enjoyed the Final State Examination which consisted of written papers in medical and surgical nursing, practical examination and oral examination by a doctor and sister tutors. I felt at ease and had no difficulty in answering the questions posed. I was even more pleased when my Sister Tutor told me that the examiners for the oral examination were very impressed with my knowledge.

Jutta had a relapse and was confined to bed. It was difficult for Betty to care for her and she suggested that I should take time off to look after Jutta. When I spoke to Miss Clarkson about that, she refused to give me leave, saying that Jutta should be in Hospital. Again I was grateful to her. Jutta's condition deteriorated. She seemed to have given up. Not only was she very ill, but her fiancé broke off their engagement and that seemed to be the last straw. Jutta was admitted to Robroyston Hospital and her health continued its downward path. It was so sad to watch her deteriorating condition.

Betty and I had to deal with another problem. The house in Belmont Street was sold and we had to move. As before, we looked for rooms and could not find anything suitable. We decided to buy a flat. This was very ambitious and fraught with difficulties, since we had no funds to support buying a flat.

We found a two-bedroom and kitchen and bathroom flat in Trefoil Avenue, Shawlands. We had no money to pay the deposit and went to the Board of Guardian (Jewish social administration) to borrow the sum of £150. They were not keen to give us the loan without a guarantor. Betty worked hard at persuading them that we would repay the loan. Eventually we did manage to find a guarantor with the help of Mr Max Doktor. He spoke to Mrs Geneen who owned the Jewish restaurant and hotel in the Gorbals, and who was, and is well-known and very generous within the community. She offered to act as guarantor for us and the Board of Guardians then gave us the loan, which we repaid in time.

We already had furniture and managed to create a nice little home for ourselves in readiness for the arrival of my mother. One of the rooms was scheduled for Jutta if and when she was to be released from hospital.


## Arrival of my Mother

My mother arrived on the 27th February 1947. Dr and Mrs MacD. went with us to Central Station to meet her. Both Betty and I were in emotional turmoil and while we were glad to have their support, we felt apprehensive and in some ways would have liked to welcome her on our own. We did not know what to expect, how to respond to her or how she would respond to us. When I left Germany I was 13 years old. I was now almost 22 years old. How would she react to two grown-up daughters? Nine years was a long time to bridge; I had grown up without her and it was difficult to visualise myself as a dutiful daughter.

The train stopped and after waiting some time, she emerged. I was quite shocked to see a very small woman when in my memory she seemed taller. She recognised us at once and was her effusive self, terribly happy to be with us, indeed to have survived and at least to have her two daughters.

We expected to see a sad and melancholic woman, but here was a very animated person ready to begin life in a strange land and willing to overcome any difficulties. She had a good sense of humour and was full of life. She had a need to talk about her experiences and we needed to know how she managed to survive.

I do not remember her carrying a case with her belongings, but do remember that she carried a brown bundle. This proved to be a blanket and in it were wrapped her limited belongings. The brown cover was a gift from HIAS (Hebrew International Aid Society). They were active in Berlin and probably other areas where Jews were in need of help. They also encouraged the survivors to prepare for Pesach by baking Matzos. My mother brought a photograph showing her and other survivors taking part in the mixing of the dough and preparing the packets of Matzos for distribution to other Jewish survivors.

*Mother with fellow survivors*

*Mother and fellow survivors baking matzos*

*Mother and fellow survivors packing matzos*

*Mother and daughters (Betty and Rosa) reunited in Glasgow in 1947*

## My mother's story—struggle to survive

After Betty left Germany on the 1st September 1939, it became obvious that there would be war and on the 3rd September 1939 Great Britain and France declared war on Germany. Hitler, in his speech to the German nation, blamed "international Judaism" for causing the war and threatened them with total destruction. The situation for the Jews became worse. While Germans were issued with ration cards they were served first. Jews too were given ration cards, but they had to wait until the Germans were served first. Usually, there was little, if any, food for them. Although the Jews were ostracized, they were forced to work in munitions factories. My mother had to work in a factory producing poisonous chemicals (poison gas?). While there, she became ill and was admitted to the St Hedwig Hospital in the Grosse Hamburger Strasse. This was a Catholic hospital and some of the nurses were nuns. She was diagnosed as having a duodenal ulcer. As part of the on-going process of removing Jews from all State institutions, the Gestapo made frequent sweeps of these institutions and whenever Jews were found, they were removed. This also applied to hospitals.

*First photo of my mother (1946) following the end of the war*

During one of these searches, a nurse took my mother out of her bed and dressed her in a nurse's gown. She was taken to a room and given instruments to clean. When the Gestapo entered the room they were told she was one of the 'Helpers'. She was saved. My mother told us that had she been taken to the Jewish Hospital in the Iranische Strasse, she would not have survived. All the Jewish patients in that Hospital were removed and transported to Poland, and did not survive.

The year was 1941 and Goebbels, the propaganda Minister, had promised Hitler that Berlin would be *"Judenrein"* (free of Jews). This led to the arrest of many Jews and during the period from 1941

83

to 1943 more than 50,000 Jews were rounded up and transported to Poland.

When she was released from the Hospital she decided the situation was extremely dangerous and decided to go underground. At first she cleared her house, then left a note stating that she was committing suicide and disappeared. She also changed her name to Lehmann and this also meant obtaining documents should she be stopped for identification. She begged her sister Erna, Jetty's mother, to join her, telling her that the Nazis were not going to resettle the Jews as they stated, but that they would be killed. Erna was by that time already exhausted and said that she could not survive living underground and because she wanted to believe the Nazis, who said that they would have food and would also be able to work, she did not resist transportation. She and her youngest daughter, Paula, sons Harry and Sally were to be deported to Riga. Her other sons—Leo and Adolf—were sent away on later transports and to Concentration camps. None of them survived.

When my mother said that her sister and her children were gassed in the train I asked her how she knew that. She then told me that she spoke to a German soldier, who was home on leave and mentioned to him that her sister and her children were on the Riga transport but had not heard from them. The soldier laughed cynically and said: "Nach Riga? They never reached Riga, they were gassed in the trains." He had taken part in that action.

She also told me that when the soldier's leave was about to end he said he could not take part in such actions. He committed suicide.

When these mass arrests and deportations took place, Jews of all ages from infants to old people were assembled and transported to Poland. The collecting point was the Old Age Home across the road from the hospital. Goebbels now claimed that Berlin was "*Judenrein*", but this was not true since there were about 1,000 Jews who lived in hiding and who survived. Most of these found refuge with friends, non-Jews, who supported them. My mother moved from place to place, never staying long in any place. Whenever she sought refuge she had to pay in gold.

She was not only in danger of betrayal from non-Jews, but even more so from informers who were Jewish and they were called "*Spitzel*" by fellow Jews. These people were promised that they and their families would not be transported to Poland and thought they could survive by informing on fellow Jews. In fact that *was* promised them, but despite that, all of their families ended up in concentration camps. Nevertheless, some of the informers did survive.

As mentioned earlier, she often did not get any rations and she was dependent on the kindness of people to give her scraps of food. One day the RAF dropped faked ration cards in order to upset the German rationing system. The order went out for good Germans to collect these and destroy them. My mother joined in, but instead of handing them in to be destroyed, she used them. At least she was able to get some food, however little, and she had to be very careful not to be caught.

The winters were very cold and the only way she could keep warm was to go to the cinema. Jews, of course, were not allowed to enter any theatres or cinemas. There were constant searches by the Gestapo, not only for Jews but also for deserters. One day when she went to the cinema a policeman spotted her, tapped her on the shoulder and warned her to disappear as the Gestapo were about to start the search. She ran to the toilet and remained there until the search was over. There were some kind people who were willing to help in many different ways.

One day as she was going downstairs in a house, a woman stopped, to ask her if Frau Goldschal lived there. Fortunately she did not know my mother nor did she have a photograph of her, but my mother knew who she was. She was a well-known Jewish informer known as the "*Blonde Gespenst*" (the blond ghost) who was responsible for the betrayal and deaths of many Jews she betrayed. My mother knew that she was an informer and quickly left the building.

(Ref. *Juden in Berlin 1938-1945* by Beate Meyer & Hermann Simon; Centrum Judaicum, Berlin 2000.)

Not only was she exposed to constant danger of betrayal, there were constant searches, not only for people but also of any cases or bags people carried. Since my mother did not live within the protection of others she had to find ways and means of getting food. The only way she could do so was to buy food on the black market. She also was fortunate in that she knew where small farm holdings were situated in and around Berlin, and she could obtain food from them. She not only had to feed herself, but she was feeding other Jews who lived in hiding. In fact, these were Jews who had escaped from various places and could not speak German and certainly not the Berlin dialect. My mother helped them to find hiding places, which were generally in bombed out buildings.

On one occasion as she was going to the subway she was stopped by the Gestapo who wanted to search her bag. She said to him: "I have no time to waste, I have to work for the Fuehrer!' He laughed and let her go. It may seem funny but to her it was really a matter of life and death. She had to keep 'cool' while, as she said, she was terrified.

Although most of the Berlin Jews had been deported, there were slave labourers working in the munitions factories. Some of them managed to escape and a number of them hid with my mother. None of them could speak German and could be easily recognised as Jews. This meant they could not get out and were dependent on my mother for food. She implored them not to go outside—not only for their own sake but also for the sake of the others. There was always the danger should they be captured, that under torture, they would betray the others. This happened on a number of occasions and it meant that my mother had to find other hiding places.

These hiding places were usually cellars, which were rat infested. By 1943/44 Berlin was severely bombed and in some ways it was easier to find hiding places in bombed-out buildings.

It should also be said that many Berliners fled the city, because of the bombing raids.

Another means of survival for her was to find work either in or near Berlin. I am not sure whether there were anti-Nazi groups who helped people like my mother.

At one time she worked for farmers, but at another time she worked as cook to a wealthy family. She told them she was a 'Sabatarian' and would not work on Saturday. They accepted that but knew only too well that she was Jewish. One day the lady of the house came to her and told her that her brother and his friends, who were high-up in the party, were coming to stay and that it would be better for her to go away and hide, since she could not protect her. There were some good people and my mother recognised that without them she could not have survived.

The bombardment of Berlin continued and food and water became even scarcer. The Russian forces had continued their drive towards Germany and stories began to reach us about the Concentration Camps and the horrors found there. When the Russians reached Berlin fierce fighting added to the further destruction of the already severely damaged city. House to house fighting took place. According to my mother, the underground railway was deliberately flooded by the Germans. Water was undrinkable and food non-existent.

Hitler committed suicide. When the fighting stopped, the Russian soldiers gave vent to their hatred and it appeared that those women who remained in Berlin throughout the fighting were at the mercy of the Russian soldiers. My mother remained in hiding until the 'elite' troops entered Berlin. These were the ones to bring some kind of order to the chaotic situation prevailing.

When she saw the cars with elite troops she came out of hiding and searched for Jewish faces among them. She approached one and said in Hebrew: *"Baruch Habah"* ("Blessed be your coming"). All he could say was: *"Du lebst?"* (You are alive?) He was most surprised that Jews had managed to survive. He believed her and took her under his protection and also gave her food.

When the American, British and French forces entered Berlin, they, together with the Russians, set up zones for each of them. While my mother was in the Russian zone, the Russian officer told her that they would be closing their zone and no one would be allowed to enter or leave. Since she had told him about Betty and me being in Britain he advised her to go into the British zone.

The remaining Jews, and those who had survived in hiding by German people, as well as those who had hidden underground, were readily accepted by the newly formed Jewish community, whose leader was Heinz Galinski, who survived the concentration camp.

When my mother approached the newly formed community, they would not believe her that she was Jewish, since they could not believe that as a Jew, she could survive on her own. She had difficulty in establishing her identity and prove that she was Jewish. Fortunately, one of the men who had lived underground under her protection vouched for her and wrote out an affidavit in Polish or Russian, witnessed and signed by a lawyer, that she was Jewish. This enabled her to register with the newly formed Jewish Community in the British zone.

Bescheinigung.

Auf Grund ihrer glaubhaften Angaben und der Bestätigung durch
den am 2.11.1892 in Kiew geborenen Vulkaniseur Simon Pressmann,
in Berlin N 65, Schulstr. 78, haben wir die Ueberzeugung gewonnen,
dass Frau Jochewed Goldsahl geb. Jungermann, geb. am 3.3.97 in
Warschau, verwitwet, Jüdin ist.

In Vertretung:

Dr. Hugo Ehrlich

*Signed affidavit that my mother was Jewish (above and below)*

Государственный союз
евреев в Германии

Удостоверение

Симон Пресман рож 2.V.1892 в Киеве
живет в Берлине Границштр. / Шулштр
дом 78 свидетельствует сим и иначе
просит, что гражданка Иохевед Голде
дан, рожденная Юнгерман фамилия
3.III 97 по национальности - еврейка.

As already mentioned, the first religious services were conducted by both the American and British Chaplains. It was there that my mother contacted two soldiers, one British and the other American. She had remembered my Edinburgh address and both of them sent me letters telling me that she was alive but was in a poor state and if I sent a food parcel to them they would make sure she would get it.

Betty and I had to contact the British commander in Berlin to make application on behalf of our mother to leave Berlin and gain permission to come to Britain. We had to promise that we would look after her and that she would not be a burden to Britain. Our application was accepted and eventually she was given a visa to enter Britain. She finally left Germany on the 27th February 1947 to start a new life in Glasgow.

**Adjusting to life in Scotland**

The next few days the reaction set in. Betty and I were working and she was left alone in the flat. She felt the cold and dampness and she was lonely. We told her about Jutta but were worried how Jutta would react to her. As for my mother, she was desperate to see her. The first visit showed us that we had no need to worry. Jutta took to her immediately and said to her: "*Wirst Du auch meine Mutti sein?*" (Will you also be my Mother?) She immediately found herself immersed in her care—visiting her and taking "Chicken soup" to her, coaxing her to eat, willing her to get better. She took Jutta to her heart and Jutta called her "*Mutti*". It was lovely to see how well they got on. My mother found a role for herself and Jutta felt at ease in her company.

At least for the last few months of Jutta's life she felt the warmth of my mother. Jutta died on the 30th June 1947 aged 24 years. Before she died she said to us, "I did not have many friends but you three were the best friends I could have had. You stood by me in time of need." My mother said the "Schema" with her. We were shattered by Jutta's death.

My mother was again very lonely and depressed and we were very concerned about her. We spoke to Dr Rushforth and she agreed with us that it was essential for her to find some work and also make contact with other Jewish people. Betty went to the Labour exchange and pleaded with them to give her a work permit. They, however, stressed the point that we had guaranteed for her entry to this country and should be able to support her. Although we did not question that, we told them that for the sake of her health, she needed to feel able and free to work and contribute to our life. Eventually she was successful and my mother obtained a work permit. At first she worked as a seamstress repairing second-hand clothing. Her employers were Mr and Mrs Simon. She was able to communicate with them in Yiddish and she began to enjoy life.

Soon after she arrived we had a visitor, also a refugee, who worked with the Refugee Children's committee. I assumed she was sent to welcome my mother or perhaps simply to meet her. She told my mother how much they, the committee, had done for me. I was very upset and asked her: "And what did you do for me?" She could not answer and my mother tried to calm me, saying, "Shush, Roselchen, I know!" I never told my mother about my life here, but she was "streetwise" and deep down understood.

One day a letter arrived addressed to my mother from the "Denazification" office in Berlin, regarding those who had been classified as Nazis and who now wanted to be reclassified as non-Nazis. Such people had to show evidence, which would show that their claim was valid. A man had claimed that he saved or helped my mother by allowing her sometimes to sleep in his home when she was destitute.

It was a very detailed questionnaire and since she was not keen to fill in the answers on her own, I helped her. Most of the questions were not problematic for her, but one question asked: "Did he demand money?" My mother exploded and shouted: *"Geld!! er verlangte Gold!"* (Money!! he demanded Gold.) She showed how he asked for it by rubbing her thumb and forefinger and saying: *"Hast Du Gold?"* ("Do you have gold?") There was a long silence and she was obviously struggling within herself how to answer that question. I finally asked how I should answer that question and eventually she said: "*Ach lass ihn leben, genug mit dem toeten, er hatte mich ja nicht verraten!!*" ("Let him be, enough of the killing, he did not betray me!!") When I asked her what I should write, she said, write "No!"

While she never knew what the decision of the Denazification Board was, I often wondered what other problems and difficulties she endured during the many years she lived that cat and mouse existence. Indeed, she said she and others who lived in hiding were called "<u>Meuser</u>" (Mice) while those Jews who were informers were called "*Spitzel*".

When the war ended and Jews came out into the open, there was great anger directed at those who betrayed other Jews to save their own lives and those of their families. However, their families often did not survive despite the promise given. According to my mother the anger of the survivors was such that they wanted to "lynch" them. However, wiser voices prevailed and the law was allowed to take its course. (Ref: *Die Juden in Berlin*, Beate Meyer & Hermann Simon, 2000. Judaicum, Berlin.)

She was keen to work in catering and approached Mrs Geneen who owned the only Jewish Hotel and Restaurant in Glasgow. Since my mother was able to cook the type of food Jewish people like, and she was good at doing that, she soon found a niche there and worked there for many years. She was a hard working woman and took part in all the functions catered by Mrs Geneen. She continued to work there until Mrs Geneen died and the Hotel/Restaurant closed.

She was nearing retiral age but was not willing to retire. The Jewish Old Age Home was looking for a cook and she applied, working there for a number of years. In fact, she was well over 70 years before she finally retired.

Retirement left her isolated and she sought work wherever she could. She was not a "club" person or interested in joining groups, but she met other lonely Jewish women and that provided her with an outlet for her own needs. She was a good listener.

# Chapter 14

## Further Training

In October 1947 I decided to train as a general nurse. I had fought against the idea and felt that the sick children's field was the most suitable one for me. I soon realised that there were limited openings as a Sick Children's nurse and reluctantly applied to Stobhill General Hospital in Springburn. Yorkhill nurses tended to move to the elite hospitals such as the Western, Royal and Victoria Infirmaries, but their training lasted 3-4 years, whilst Stobhill's, which was a local authority hospital, lasted $2^1/_2$ years. In my interview with the Matron I was asked if I would be able to manage the course in General Nursing. This was surely a strange question; after all, I had successfully completed the Sick Children's Nursing course, which I still consider quite a challenging one. (It took me many years later to recognize that there was a struggle within the different types of nursing.)

In 1948 the National Health Service was established. Prior to that, hospitals were either governed by private companies or the local Authority. In the "private" hospitals, people tended to contribute small sums either as individuals or through the workplace. Beds and wards were endowed, therefore the funds were adequate. Since they were also teaching hospitals they tended to be better equipped and more advanced than the local Authority hospitals. No patient was ever refused admission. With the advent of the National Health Service, funding was shared between hospitals in a Health Authority and while many improvements were made it also developed into a more bureaucratic organisation.

When I started at Stobhill it was still under the control of Glasgow Corporation but with the establishment of the National Health Service, it became part of it. It started life as a Poor/Work House and that stigma was to remain for many years. However, I found the nursing care there was better than that achieved in the elite hospitals. This was evidenced when patients were transferred for prolonged care to Stobhill and it was not unusual for these patients to have bedsores. Stobhill had many long-stay patients and rarely would one see pressure sores. Since I was a post-registered nurse, I started in the second year. The lectures there were much the same as in Yorkhill; the system was also much the same.

My first ward experience was a female psychiatric ward. I found this ward very traumatic. There were forty women in the ward of varying ages and conditions. I thought I would use what I had learned from Dr Rushworth during my psycho-analysis, but soon realised that some of the suggestions could have a detrimental effect on me. The emphasis was to put oneself in the position of the patient. This, I believe now, to be quite dangerous. One can show understanding and compassion but to attempt a deeper immersion in the state of mind of the patient is dangerous. We were also short-staffed. On several occasions I was left alone in the ward with only a domestic worker. The wards were locked and if help was needed it was difficult to obtain that. One day, one of the patients became very agitated and very difficult to control. She tried to throw me out of the window. It was a most frightening situation and left a deep impression on me.

Betty married in 1948 and my mother and I moved to Shields Road into rented rooms. It was not ideal but we had our own kitchen and each a bedroom. I gave my share of the flat to Betty and Henry as a wedding present. Later we moved into lodgings in McCulloch Street. It was not satisfactory either, but had to do until we had enough money to buy a flat.

On the whole I enjoyed the training in Stobhill, but was glad when I completed it in 1949. I remained there working on night duty as a staff nurse in theatre. This was a new system since up till then, theatre staff had to be "on call" for any night theatre. This way it allowed some of the day staff a full night's sleep. After three months I decided to move on and opted to take midwifery training. I applied to Ayrshire Central Maternity Hospital.

The midwifery training consisted of two six-month periods. The first part enabled one to practice under supervision while on completion of the second part, the midwife could work in an independent capacity, provided the pregnancy and labour were normal.

I enjoyed the first part and gained good experience. Irvine had a poor population and many people lived in squatters' camps. These were disused army camps consisting of Nissen Huts. Not ideal for homes but it was shelter of a kind and people created a liveable environment.

After passing my examinations, I applied to the Southern General Hospital for the second part of the training. The main reason for that was that Ayrshire Central Hospital had limited places for district deliveries and Glasgow was therefore more likely to give me the experience I required. Each of us had to have ten home deliveries. While we had our lectures and labour room experience at the Maternity unit, for district work we were attached to the district midwifery service at Montrose Street. I very much enjoyed the experience, had excellent cases and became quite confident in that role. I was asked to continue as a district Midwife on completion of my training but felt that I needed more experience within a hospital before becoming a district midwife.

I therefore applied to Redlands Hospital for Women. This was a small hospital in the west end of Glasgow. It was opened and run by women doctors and had, apart from general wards, also a gynaecological unit and a separate house providing maternity services. Both buildings had been private houses and were converted to suit its functions.

The maternity house had no lift and the patients had to be carried up and down broad winding stairs! Two rooms downstairs were for antenatal cases and two rooms upstairs for post-natal cases, plus a nursery and two labour rooms with a total of three beds. Any patient requiring surgery i.e. caesarean section, had to be carried outside, placed on a trolley, wheeled to the main building and then carried up the stairs into the building.

What I liked about this set up was that as a midwife I could work in any of the sections, from antenatal clinic, ward, labour rooms, nursery, postnatal care and therefore gain experience in all areas. At the same time I knew the patients from the beginning of pregnancy to the delivery and aftercare. Working in a large teaching hospital, one tended to be isolated in one section and therefore the experience gained would have been limited. I stayed there for almost two years and then decided to move further afield. During that time my mother and I bought a flat in Cartha Street, Shawlands. By 1952 my mother was now well established and settled in and I felt ready to move on in my career. When I discussed with my mother that I was interested to go to Israel, she readily accepted it. Betty lived close-by should my mother need help.

# Chapter 15

## Israel 1952-1954

Israel was established on the 8th May 1948. The War of Independence placed a tremendous burden on the young State. It was attacked on all sides, except from the sea. Despite all the odds against it, Israel was successful in defeating the attacking forces. Not only was the war a great burden, there were many Jews who had to be rescued from the chaos in Europe and indeed elsewhere. The burden, in economic as well as social terms, was enormous. Jews came from Europe, North Africa, Yemen and other Middle East countries. It became a melting pot of peoples, languages and cultures.

While hospitals and clinics existed, these were primarily run by Kupath Cholim (Health Insurance, part of the Histadruth (Trades Union)). The new government took over those hospitals, which had been part of the Mandatory Government, primarily military hospitals. These had to be staffed and equipped and a call went out for doctors and nurses including midwives. I now felt ready to go to Israel and give my support as a midwife.

It took some time to cut through the bureaucracy that was Israel. I left Britain at the beginning of December 1952. As it happened, Chaim Weizmann, the first President of Israel, had died and the plane I was to travel on was delayed waiting for his son from the US to join the flight. It was a good flight and I felt excited by the prospect in taking part in the life of Israel. While waiting for my visa I took lessons in Hebrew so that I could communicate more readily. I already knew the rudiments of modern Hebrew from school in Germany but since it was a long time ago, I felt it to be necessary to re-learn it.

Henry had a cousin in Israel and he had written to her to tell her of my intention to work in Israel. She asked if I could bring car parts, which were difficult to obtain in Israel. Anita and Asher were very helpful when I arrived in Israel.

The plane landed early in the morning and I felt very emotional. Although I had not been brought up in a Zionist environment, nor had I taken part in any activity which was identified with Israel, I had felt a strong bond with Israel. I believed that Israel was essential for Jewish survival and also to provide some protection against the many anti-Jewish sentiments and activities. It was fast becoming the melting pot of Jewish life and culture and it needed the support of Diaspora Jewry.

I was met by a representative of the Israel Health Ministry, who wanted me to go to Tiberias. Although I had been given to understand that I would be working at Sarafand, I did not mind, nor did I know any better, and was willing to go wherever I was needed.

I knew that Asher was working at Lod (now Ben Gurion) Airport in the aircraft repair workshop. I told the lady that I had car parts for Asher and I wanted to see him first. She did not object. When Asher came he was most friendly and when told that I was to travel on to Tiberias, he was most annoyed and told the lady that it was not right to send me to Tiberias, which he considered not suitable to begin with. He felt that I should acclimatise first for a week, and then begin work. She agreed. It was my first contact with bureaucracy in Israel and to learn how people dealt with officialdom.

I spent the first week with Anita and Asher, received a ration book and after settling in I was keen to start work. After some correspondence with the Nursing Department of the Health Ministry, it was decided that I should start in Sarafand.

On arriving at the hospital I was interviewed by the Head Nurse, Mrs Nasa. On my application form I had provided all the necessary information regarding professional qualification and experience. I had also indicated that I was interested in continuing to work in Midwifery.

Sarafand was a big hospital, which had been a British Military Hospital adjacent to the big Army Camp. It was now a Government Hospital used for civilian purposes. It catered for adult medical and surgical patients, had two children's wards and a little annexe for premature babies, a maternity unit, two wards for male and female tuberculosis patients and a purpose-built unit for post-poliomyelitis children. The children were affected by the world-wide outbreak of Poliomyelitis. Most of the hospital consisted of separate military-type huts but the post-polio unit was built with the help of WHO, which also provided physiotherapists.

Mrs Nasa was desperately in need of trained Sick Children's Nurses. There was no such training in Israel. It did not take much to persuade me to work in that capacity and I was allocated to one of the wards. Ilana, who was a trained nursery nurse, was in charge of that ward and overall responsibility rested with Miriam Braun who had trained in Israel as a nursery nurse.

The ward was a mixed medical and surgical ward, dealing with burns, usual operations such as appendicitis, but had also a room for children suffering from diphtheria. Since the disease was almost absent in Britain, this was a new experience for me. Every child required a tracheostomy and these were carried out in one of the small rooms off the main ward.

The chief of the ward was English; the other doctors came from Hungary, Romania and Czechoslovakia. Since most of them spoke English the visits were conducted in English. I remained in that ward for a few months to settle in and was then given another ward. Here the chief was Austrian and the rest came from various countries. The ward visits were conducted in either German, English, or Hebrew.

The nursing staff consisted of people from many different countries. Some came from Russia, Romania, Austria, Persia (Iran), Hungary and Morocco. All had very traumatic experiences and each coped with them in their own specific ways. We also had student nurses. They were supernumerary and the training was based on the American system.

The ward held 35-40 children but during the winter months it could reach almost 50. The children came from the towns and villages around the hospital and included both Jewish and Arab children. Parents were not allowed into the wards and visiting time was simply asking about the children while standing at one of the ward's windows. One had to watch in case mothers came in to breast-feed their children, particularly if the child was beyond that type of feeding and the mothers had no milk. Another problem was that many parents, particularly those from Yemen, had many children and they often did not know which of them was in hospital.

Children were sent home but little guidance was given to mothers on how to care for their children, particularly infants. At that time there were also not enough social workers to give support. However, I had one opportunity to give some guidance to one mother. Her young child had been suffering from Kwashiorkor, a syndrome produced by severe deficiency of protein. Treatment was successful and the child was considered well enough to go home. The doctor suggested that I should give the mother a leaflet with examples of suitable foods to give her child. I did not agree with that suggestion and felt that it would be better for the mother to come to the ward and see what type of meals we gave and also how to prepare the meals.

The doctor was aghast at that idea, considering the mothers too stupid and made other unsubstantiated comments about them. After some argument he gave in to my suggestion and I asked the mother to come to the ward. She was very keen to do so and when she came I gave her a gown and explained to her what the purpose of this exercise was. She looked after her little girl and fed her. Two days later she came to me and said, "Sister, there are so many babies here to feed, could I not help?" I was delighted. She learned how to change nappies, the importance of washing hands and general cleanliness and sat with the nurses feeding babies, apart from feeding her child. The doctor was duly impressed and I felt vindicated and also taught him a lesson, in that it is wrong to judge people simply on the basis that they came from less advanced societies. She was intelligent and a quick learner.

Throughout my time in Israel I continued to take Hebrew lessons. The student nurses, many of who came from displaced or concentration camps and had to learn Hebrew, received lessons as part of the course and the Hebrew teacher gave me lessons after my duty finished. I became quite fluent and all my reports were written in Hebrew.

I did make grammatical mistakes sometimes, and children were quick to correct me. For example, I had addressed little Dalia in the Hebrew masculine form and she was very quick in telling me. "I am called Dalia," she said snootily. I apologised profusely.

This little girl had been admitted with a diagnosis of peritonitis. I asked the mother why she waited so long before getting help. She replied: "The Rabbi was away in Paris." I could not understand why she did not get a doctor. When I asked what the Rabbi was doing there, she replied that he was collecting funds for their community. They sent a telegram to him asking him what to do. He sent one back to tell them to get a doctor, which they did and the little girl was admitted. It occurred to me then that she and the other members of that community had been survivors from a camp and were unable to make decisions and very much dependent on the Rabbi.

I had a lot to learn.

I mentioned that many of my staff were severely traumatised by their experiences and on occasions difficulties arose. For example, the nurses came to me to complain about Chava. She evidently did not feed the babies but walked about the ward singing to herself. I had been aware of Chava's behaviour, but in honesty did not know how to help her. When I eventually spoke to her and explained to her the need to pull her weight, she replied, "Rosalie, when I see a baby with an infusion I must watch it in case the drip stops and the baby dies." I suggested to her that perhaps she should feed a baby while sitting and watching the drip, if that gave her reassurance. It worked well and Chava also seemed less stressed.

During the busy winter months another ward was opened and I took charge of that one too. The experience was excellent. Not only did I learn to live in a very mixed environment, with many different types of people, but also became much more understanding to their problems and needs.

All the charge nurses took it in turns to take responsibility of the hospital during the night and I did too. This gave me greater insight into the hospital's total problems. Staff complement, dealing with emergencies and supporting nursing staff. Cultural differences had also to be accommodated; for example, where to accommodate the many relatives who came with a patient. This happened more with Bedouins, who lived far away. One Ward was empty and so they were allowed to sleep there. I hoped that they would not light a fire in the ward—the result would have been horrific. These were all wooden frames and fire extinguishers were almost non-existent. Those which could be found were difficult to remove from the rusty nails holding them.

My free time was spent with Anita and Asher or with Muriel Links in Tel-Aviv. I made friends with the physiotherapist and when we were on leave, travelled in her Morris Minor to Safed. I was able to explain to her about the history of the Jews and what I knew of the land of Israel. We both enjoyed the trip and got on very well. Jetty was also in Israel for one year. She stayed at a Kibbutz near Haifa (Tel Yitzchak) and I spent some time with her. She also came to Tel-Aviv and we also spent a weekend in Jerusalem.

I had a sense of religious freedom, which I cherished. While I am not orthodox I feel a bond with and towards the philosophy of Judaism. There was also a feeling that we shared a common bond despite the fact that most of the people came from such different backgrounds. People were enthusiastic in making a success of the new State. There were many difficulties, some economical, others to do with defence and the balancing of a population, so diverse. Since the hospital was adjacent to the main army camp I was very much aware of any military movement and the sound of tanks moving out of the camp. We were in fact in an area, which was only 10 kilometres wide between the Mediterranean Sea and the West Bank. One could easily lose one's way across no-man's land and the dangers that posed. We once had to be rescued when we found ourselves in such a situation.

I felt part of the life in Israel and was impressed by the efforts people made in making the State work. There was a constant influx of Jews either from Europe or the Arab countries. Many were very poor, requiring housing and some means of earning a living. The young State could barely cope. In addition it had to build an army, air force and navy and be constantly on the alert of attacks. These were frequent and always led to reprisals and blood-shed.

The newcomers had to be integrated into the culture and norms of Israel, and the educational system, in particular the army, played a most important part. It was fascinating watching this process. When I first arrived in Israel it was quite frightening how aggressive some of the men were, particularly those coming from North Africa. While waiting for a bus to take us to Sarafand, there was always a stampede to get on to the bus. If the men did not get their way, they were quick to draw knives. They were undisciplined and would not wait their turn. Within six month I was able to notice a change in their behaviour. If anyone jumped the queue, it was they who would make sure that they did not succeed, but without the use of knives.

The military forces consisted of conscripted men and women. Indeed it was already then a "citizen force" where everyone of military age had to undergo military training and be ready at very short notice to answer the call to arms. To test this, there were regular emergency call-ups when each member had to respond to given signals. It was quite an achievement but also caused havoc in industry and hospitals, when men and women suddenly disappeared. Those not called up just had to get on with whatever they were doing.

Other observations of change in attitudes and behaviour were in the attitude to work and religious practices. Men and boys from very orthodox families wore "Payes" or sidelocks. In my ward I had boys who came from Yemenite homes where this too was the practice. Following a day off-duty, I noticed that one of the boys, Schmuel by name, was minus his "Payes" and when I asked him who cut them off, he replied, "I did." I thought that the boys had bullied him and forced him to cut off his Payes. When I questioned them about their behaviour, they assured me that this was not the case. This was only clear when Schmuel spoke up and, pointing to the other boys in the room, said, pointing to each of them, "He is a Jew and I am a Jew too. They do not have Payes, therefore I too will not have one." When I asked him what his parents would say to that, he replied, "What does it matter, I want to be like them!" The parents accepted it.

Sarafand hospital served the surrounding small towns, villages and communal farms. It had also a number of transit camps for Yemenite, Algerian and Moroccan Jews as well as Arabs and Bedouins. One saw a wide variety of behaviours and child-care practices. It was surprising to see Jews engaging in witchcraft. For example, babies were admitted suffering from gastro-enteritis with burn wounds around the umbilicus. When asked who did this, we were told it was done to drive out the evil spirits. I saw new-born babies with tetanus as a result of infection through the umbilical cord. These babies were delivered at home under very poor hygienic conditions.

Our task was not only to treat the children but to educate the mothers. Because of the great poverty and ignorance of child-care, not only where basic hygiene was concerned but also effective nutrition, particularly infants, it was difficult to ensure that the children would be cared for effectively. Indeed once the children were ready to go home, the parents would not take them back. We had to call in the police to escort the children to their homes and ensure that the parents accepted them. As the community nursing service became established, more effective help was available. Gradually these people were given proper houses and the men work, which helped to improve their circumstances. It must be said that the mothers were keen to learn and ready to accept methods of infant and child care which were outwith their experience.

I became quite fluent in Hebrew and had no difficulty in conversing. All my reports were written in Hebrew. I went to theatres and concerts and visited Kibbutzim. I had always wanted to be able to play the violin and once I received my pay (after three months) I arranged violin lessons with a member of the Israeli Philharmonic Orchestra. I bought a violin and was now all set. I was allowed to use one of the storerooms for practicing and enjoyed that. I never reached any level of competence, but did enjoy the challenge.

Anita and others tried hard to get me married off, but all their efforts were in vain. I was not really ready to build up a lasting relationship with a man and was considered a "cold fish". I had other plans and hopes. I did get a proxy proposal of marriage once. This occurred while travelling back from Tel-Aviv to Sarafand. A man sitting beside me in the bus decided that I should be his son's wife. When I asked him how old the son was, he said that he was 18 years old. He had no trade or profession. I told him that I would be too old for him but that did not seem to matter to him. I was by that time nearly 27 years old. I suggested to him that his son should first of all learn a trade and become independent, and also be allowed to choose his wife himself. He was very polite and thanked me for advising him.

My first roommate was Ada. She came from London. She was in charge of the female tuberculosis ward and had been in Israel for two years. She was a vivacious girl and much in demand by the opposite sex. We got on well together. Unfortunately she left to return home to be with her mother who was dying. She never returned to Israel and got married in London.

My next roommate was Miriam. She originally came from Germany and left with her mother to settle in Palestine. When the Mandate ended her mother married a British policeman and the three left for New Zealand. The marriage was not a success. Miriam trained as a nurse in New Zealand but always yearned to return, to what became, Israel. She had fallen in love with Yitzchak who originally came from Turkey, and they corresponded throughout her stay in New Zealand. In 1953 she returned to Israel to resume her friendship. Her mother remained in New Zealand. Miriam worked in my ward, shared a room and we became friends. Since I was older she looked upon me as an older sister and I supported her during her rather stormy emotional period. Yitzchak proposed to her but Miriam could not make up her mind. Added to the tumult was the fact that her aunt, Miss Hoschander, was against the marriage. She felt there was too great a cultural barrier and that the marriage would not last. I was in the middle. I had my reservations too and discussed it with Miriam, but in the end it was her decision.

The eve of Yom Haatsmauth (independence day) Miriam went through an emotional crisis and felt that she could not leave Israel again. Her relationship with Yitzchak intensified and eventually they married. Her aunt was not happy and blamed me for not influencing Miriam against the marriage. Initially their marriage was a happy one and they had three boys, but Miriam's frustration with Yitzchack eventually led to their separation. She was very ambitious and could not understand his reluctance to improve his position as a diamond cutter. She also showed little understanding for his problems and was not supportive during his last illness.

The news from home also indicated that there were problems. Henry became more and more disturbed and my mother's arthritis became very troublesome. I was asked to become Head Nurse (Matron) of a maternity hospital in Tiberias but was torn between that and returning home. Betty became pregnant and Maurice was born in October 1954. There were many problems at home and I felt it was wrong to leave Betty to cope on her own.

I had also decided to go into teaching and for that I would require to return to Britain. I therefore decided to return to Britain and left Israel in December 1954.

# Chapter 16

## Return to Glasgow: New Professional Role

I left Israel by ship, travelling to Marseilles. The crossing was extremely rough and everyone on the ship was seasick. Mount Etna was erupting. We arrived in Naples early in the morning. The sky was grey and it was very cold. We were taken by bus to Pompeii. The weather conditions made the setting very eerie. Pompeii was empty of people and only the ruins were there and the feeling of devastation was intense. Returning many years later in the summer made me realise that my first impressions were a truer one, more representative of the tragedy caused by the eruption of Vesuvius.

We continued our journey by ship to Marseilles. I had to go to the bank to collect some money. We were not allowed to take any money out of Israel so I had asked my mother to transfer some to Marseilles. I nearly missed the train to Paris. This was partly due to the unhelpfulness of the railway staff. However, I managed to join the others from the ship and we all travelled together to Paris.

I was soon made aware of the anti-Jewish feelings in France. The ticket inspector/collector found an error in the ticket of one of our members. He insisted that she left the train. He would not allow her to continue. Since I had some money now I offered to pay the difference, but he refused to accept it. She was very worried because she had to make a connection at Brest for the journey to the USA. There was no reasoning with the Frenchman and it was then that we became very aggressive. There was no justification for the railway official's behaviour and we decided to deal with him. One of the boys held him against the window and threatened to throw him out unless he accepted the offer and allowed the woman to continue. He called us "dirty Jews", but we showed him that times had changed and that we would not allow him to intimidate us.

He was most surprised at our behaviour and obviously frightened, so quickly gave in. No one else made any attempt to interfere with us.

We arrived in Paris, and because I was not feeling very well, I stayed in Paris for a few days before moving on to London. While in London I stayed with Ada for a few days and then continued my journey to Glasgow.

My mother was suffering a great deal of pain and found walking very difficult. I decided to seek medical help for her and made an appointment for her to be seen privately. The doctor's view was that it was anxiety due to her experiences in Germany. I would not accept that. Indeed this approach to survivors was typical of many doctors at the time. We decided to change to another NHS practice doctor called Dr Glasser, who was more understanding to my mother's problems. He made an appointment for her to see a consultant at the Royal Infirmary, Glasgow, who advised deep X-ray treatment which proved to be very effective and her improvement in walking and relief from pain enabled her to go back to work and enjoy life.

Henry was very depressed and obsessive. Betty and Henry lived on the top floor in Trefoil Avenue and it was very difficult to pull the pram up and down the stairs. Eventually Betty and Henry bought a terraced house in Titwood Road which made life easier for them.

I decided to remain in Paediatric Nursing and went to the labour office dealing with professional posts. Yorkhill Hospital was looking for a ward sister. I applied and was accepted as ward sister in ward 5, a medical ward, and started work there on the 1st February 1955.

It was a time of change. The old attitudes were changing. Nurses became more assertive and parents began to question more. Israel had taught me a great deal and I was able to take these changes on board. I started ward tutorials for nurses and took an active part in teaching at ward level. I had a good relationship with doctors and nurses and also took an active part in introducing change.

Although I discussed the need for children to be allowed greater mobility at ward level and have play facilities, I was never included in discussions to implement these changes. We were always short-staffed and had little time to supervise play or read to the children and I had suggested to Dr Stone, who by then was the Psychiatrist at the hospital, that nursery nurses might be useful for that type of work.

While some years later nursery nurses were employed, they were not used for the work they had been trained for and that was always a bone of contention for me. In fact, they were used as 'nurses' and like so many other new grades, which were gradually introduced, the nurses' role and value were severely undermined. My opinion was that once a two-tier system was introduced, the dividing line would become blurred, and fewer registered nurses would be required. It was in fact a form of 'cheap labour'.

Another important change was the introduction of extended visiting and eventually free visiting. This meant quite an adjustment in ward routine and management. Nurses were now much more open to scrutiny by parents and both parents and nurses were unsure of their roles. It was a time of adjustment and there were periods of friction. The relative calm and order, which had been the norm, was no longer observed.

In addition to those changes, the children were now receiving school lessons. This was under the control of the Education Authorities, but it too produced tension between nurses and teachers. I did not have any difficulties in accepting the presence of the teachers and their roles and mine were readily identified. We both worked together for the benefit of the children. If any child had a problem with lessons, the teacher would always discuss it with me so that we could help the child. The teacher also understood that I, as the ward sister, would decide which child was fit enough for lessons and that was accepted. This was not the case with most of the wards where a great deal of conflict arose.

The ward was to be renovated and therefore closed and I was moved to the admissions hall, nowadays the accident and emergency department. I had decided to become a nurse teacher and had applied to the University of Edinburgh where the first course in Scotland was held. I was not accepted primarily because I did not have a background in science subjects. I started to take classes in chemistry in the hope that eventually I would be accepted. Eventually I was accepted for the course at the Royal College of Nursing in London and started the course in 1957. Unfortunately I did not complete it. I had emotional problems and felt that I had to give support to Betty and Henry. Henry was admitted to Crichton Royal in Dumfries and Betty was left with Maurice. She had little income. My mother required deep x-ray treatment for osteo-arthritis. I felt that I should be with them at that difficult time. I returned to Yorkhill in 1958 and started to work as an unqualified nurse tutor. I enjoyed that but, of course, was very frustrated at the lack of a proper qualification.

I had been introduced to a number of men but had no interest in any of them. In January 1959, a little matchmaking took place. I, along with Betty and Henry, were invited to Mary Finkel's home. As usual, I was reluctant to go, but since I knew Mary and Mendel Plotkin (Mendel was Mary Finkel's brother) and I had delivered one of Mary's daughters, I went too.

Also invited were Joe and his sisters. I thought that he was married to one of them and did not pay much attention to him. It was a pleasant evening and when it was time to go home, Mendel would not take me in his car but said that Joe would take me in his car. I then began to realise that there was a plot afoot. Joe took me home and asked me out after explaining to me that the young ladies with him were his sisters.

I gradually got to know him better and felt at ease with him. He was gentle and kind and we felt we had something in common. Courting was interrupted when he went on tropical trials for several months. We corresponded and on his return continued the relationship. After a short courtship we got engaged, in October 1959, and decided to marry in December. Joe was 36 and I was 34. We were both mature enough to realise the pitfalls of marriage. He had a flat, which was rented and had been his parents, and therefore there was no need to wait. We had little savings but we both were working so could save some money and eventually buy a house.

While both my mother and Betty were pleased, somehow there was some resentment on Betty's part. I had always been very supportive to her and she felt that our relationship would change and she would have less of my support. The relationship was bound to change but there was no reason why we could not remain close and give each other support. From the very beginning there were tensions between our families and Betty found it difficult to accept that I now had another family and that there must be some sharing. This tension spoiled the approach to my wedding and indeed the wedding itself.

# Chapter 17

## Joe's Story and His Background

I was the youngest in a family of five. There were three boys and two girls. The eldest was Kitty who was born in 1911. Benny was born in 1914. Wolfie was born in 1918. Rosie was born in 1920 and I was born in 1923.

My family originated from a little village called Vinerod in the Ukraine. My brothers and sisters knew very little of the life there, except that the family lived in a small village whose population was mainly Jewish. They spoke Yiddish and had little education. My father was a cap maker and my mother's role was primarily as a wife and mother. It was a close-knit community and life was lived within this narrow religious community.

The origins of the Jews living in the Ukraine or any other part of the world can be traced back to the dispersal. While it is difficult to be absolutely accurate, enough historical data is available to get a reasonably clear picture of the movement of Jews and where they eventually settled.

There were two main routes by which Jews moved to the region. One was from Persia into Khazaria, north of the Caspian Sea. Khazaria was heathen but in 700AD its King converted to Judaism and it became a Jewish Kingdom from 700-1016AD. Many Jews settled there and although there is no trace of the Khazarians, historians describe the life there as tolerant to other religions. Russia attacked and defeated the kingdom and the Jews moved into Russia.

The other route was via Germany. Many Jews had settled in Germany. Throughout their stay in many towns and cities they were subjected to persecution and expulsions. Refugees fled to the east from Germany in 1069 and continued throughout the 12th, 13th and 14th centuries. They spoke German and over the centuries this developed into the Yiddish language, which became the accepted means of communication between Jews throughout Europe.

Another way of determining the origins of people is by their names. In biblical times the offspring were known as "Ben" or "Bat", the Hebrew for "Son" or "Daughter" of... Gradually that changed and people's names reflected where they lived and their work. In Germany and Austria, city names were often chosen. In many cases names were imposed on people, which were insulting and derogatory. In Russia, too, Jews were made to follow the pattern of personal names as it already existed for the non-Jewish population. It is difficult to place the name Sacharin. One reason is that it too had changed as far as spelling is concerned. When my parents arrived in this country, they had no birth certificates and could not write Roman script. The immigration official wrote down the names as he heard it. I believe originally it was spelt as Sakharin or Zakharin.

Wherever Jews lived they were subjected to attacks and the Jews of the Ukraine too had their share of brutal persecution and destruction. As a result of one such pogrom in 1913, when most of the family was killed, my parents and two-year-old Kitty left the Ukraine and paid to travel to the US. The owners of the ship and the captain could not have been very honest. Instead of travelling to the US they were landed in England, but were told that it was the US. They were not to know otherwise.

They stayed in London for a short while and then moved to Glasgow. Instead of travelling by train, they were told the best way to travel was by boat. It was a long and rough journey for them but eventually they arrived in Glasgow and made their home in the Gorbals where a large number of Jews lived, who had come to Britain in previous immigrations.

Living conditions were very difficult as the housing stock was in a poor state. Many tenements did not have inside toilets. Their flat consisted of one room with an outside toilet. There was no bath and no hot water. By the time I was born, seven people shared these accommodations and sleeping arrangements were unsatisfactory. My father, Benny and Wolfie, slept on a bed made up from chairs. Since there was no bathroom, the children were bathed in a tin bath every night filled from kettles of hot water.

Moving to another flat was also a problem because factors were very unwilling to rent houses to Jews. While there was no open anti-Semitism and no attacks on Jews, there were covert acts against the Jews in that they had difficulties in renting and buying houses and in some occupations, Jews were not encouraged to join. However, they did manage to rent a flat in Norfolk Street, also in the Gorbals. This flat had a room and kitchen with an inside toilet, but no bath or hot water. My parents slept in the kitchen, which had a recess for a double bed. Benny and Wolfie slept in a cupboard bed, which most houses had at that time. I shared a sofa bed with Kitty and Rosie. This could be closed during the day.

My father was a cap maker and he found work in that field. To make ends meet he also worked in the evenings and on Sundays. My mother initially also worked as a seamstress, while a distant relation looked after Kitty.

While my parents did not have a secular education, my father had a good grasp of mathematical concepts. For example, the *Sunday Express* published cartoons which had problems in them. My father always solved these problems mentally, basically using algebra, which he never even knew existed. My mother had a tremendous amount of common sense and was able to solve many of the problems of daily living.

Despite the poverty, we were always clean and neatly dressed. They were caring parents and had a philosophy that parents should never knowingly do anything to shame or embarrass their children. We, as children, were also taught that we should not knowingly do anything to shame or embarrass our parents. When Kitty started school and was able to read, she helped my parents to understand English and since she also spoke Yiddish, she also undertook to read and write letters for them.

We all attended Gorbals Primary School and progressed well. Indeed, the teachers used to visit my parents, coming after school, joining us for a cup of tea and enjoying talking to my parents. Teachers were highly regarded, being "educated", while the majority of the parents did not have basic school education. While Jews were able to read and write Hebrew, they were unable to do so in English. Kitty was a good scholar and for her secondary education attended Queens Park School. Benny, Wolfie and Rosie went to Strathbungo Higher Grade School.

About 1933 we moved to 856 Pollokshaws Road. This was a bigger flat, which had two bedrooms, a lounge and a large kitchen with a full bathroom. I transferred to Shawlands Academy.

Kitty eventually went to Glasgow University, but failed to get a degree. She started private tutoring and continued working in that field for nine years, when she left for London to work for the Zionist movement. She had been active in Poale Zion in Glasgow for many years. Benny left school at 14 years of age, the school-leaving age at that time. Wolfie was dux of the year and left to enter service at a lawyer's office and after passing the local government examination, joined the then Glasgow Corporation housing department. Rosie began work in an office.

**Life during the War**

When war broke out in September 1939, I was evacuated to Annan in Dumfriesshire. I was in the third year at school, and because of the evacuation, different pupils were allocated at Annan. I had to drop science and continued with French (the second language), started in the second year. The first language was Latin. I remained in Annan for 5 months, during which time my parents did not come to see me. They could not afford to travel and there were also travel restrictions. Kitty visited me once.

Gradually everyone moved back to Glasgow and I continued at Shawlands with French. During 1940 and 1941 there were bombing raids. At Pollokshaws Road, we all congregated in one house on the ground floor and we were there most nights. A landmine destroyed the corner building at Deanston Drive and James Gray Street, killing the majority of people there. Another landmine destroyed a building in Nelson Street in the Gorbals, both equidistant from our home. In Scotland the worst bombing of the war was at Clydebank, not all that far away as the crow flies.

Wolfie went into the Army in 1939 joining the Seaforth Highlanders, and Benny, who was not considered medically fit to join the Army, became an ambulance driver.

I sat my Highers in 1941 obtaining 4 Highers in Latin, French, Maths and English and a lower in History. That was the maximum one could do at that time. It was a group certificate, which meant that if you failed one, you failed the lot, unless there were exceptional circumstances.

I decided to go to University to study Naval Architecture. I had an interview with the Dean of the Faculty of Engineering. Science was a prerequisite for entry into the Faculty and I did not have it. However, he said he quite liked the fact that I had a "classical" education and I was accepted. He suggested that I try to get a job in a shipyard (since it was a "sandwich" course).

I wrote to a number of yards on the Clyde but very few were interested in Degree students. However, one reply from Fairfield in Govan asked me for an interview, which was successful. I started work in Govan, receiving 7/6d per week (under 40p) and that included Saturday morning. In those days there were no grants. I applied for a Carnegie bursary which paid part of the fees. My parents had no money and could not give me financial support. I found the first year very difficult. I knew virtually nothing about Physics and Chemistry. However, I passed the first degree examinations in Mathematics, Chemistry and Technical Drawings, failed in Physics but passed on resit.

## WARTIME EXPERIENCE
### Royal Navy 1943-1946

Although I was in a reserved occupation, which meant I was doing essential war work, I had been thinking about joining the Navy and did so in 1943.

I joined the Royal Navy in June 1943. I went to HMS *Collingwood* at Fareham in Hampshire for my basic training. The train journey to London at that time usually took more than 20 hours. The first or second night after I arrived, a bomb fell on one of the huts, so the night was spent sifting through the rubble for survivors.

After basic training I was drafted to a transit camp at Stockheath nearby. This was a large tented camp, and because of the blackout, if someone came back late at night, he would usually look for the first tent which had some space in it, and would sleep there. There was a big crowd of us, and one of the officers asked if anyone had a school certificate. I was the only one who stepped forward. The officer wanted to know the subjects taken. The procedure was to look at the notice board every morning to see if our names appeared for draft. When I looked at the board the following morning, my name appeared to take charge of an outside working party of six, to collect picks and shovels, to dig trenches about a mile away. We would march along the road in single file, very often singing "Heigh Ho, heigh ho, it's off to work we go", just like the seven dwarfs in 'Snow White'. Fortunately, this did not last long and I was drafted to Force J2.

This was a combined operations group, firstly at Wyke Regis in Dorset where some of us were billeted at Wyke House, and then moved to Weymouth, Dorset, which was a base for motor torpedo boats and motor gunboats (MTBs & MGBs). I went 2 or 3 times a week to the Naval Base at Portland Bill for revolver practice. We had Smith and Wesson 38s and/or Webley 45s. I took part in a practice landing near Swanage, and did guard duty at the Alexandra Palace Hotel, where plans were being prepared for the invasion. I had wanted to go to sea and saw the Commanding Officer. He recommended me for a commission, which meant that I would have to do some sea-time.

I was drafted to Newcastle to join a Tribal Class Destroyer, HMS *Nubian*. She was being repaired there as she had been damaged in the Tunisian Campaign. We were attached to Western Approaches Command and operated in the Channel and the North Atlantic (based at Milford Haven or Greenock). We escorted troopships, such as the *Queen Mary*, *Queen Elizabeth*, *Empress of Britain* and other former liners, about 500 miles into the Atlantic, where we left them to continue on their own, as they were fast and could outrun any U-Boat, unless one was already in the area. We would wait around to pick up another ship and escort it to Greenock or Milford Haven. We were also attached to the Home Fleet, based at Scapa Flow, as Arctic Patrol, which included mainly the Faroe Islands, where we sometimes anchored in Skalfjord, North Cape (Norway), and as far north as Bear Island and the Barents Sea, which is part of the Arctic Ocean. We also took part in most of the strikes against the *Tirpitz*, anchored in Altenfjord, Norway, escorting Aircraft Carriers, Battleships and Cruisers. One escort carrier, *Nabob*, was torpedoed, but not sunk.

Life on board a Destroyer was very hard. The mess decks usually had about a foot of water sloshing about. This was mainly due to the ammunition chutes on the upper deck being open. We were not allowed to sling hammocks at sea, because in the event of being sunk, a properly lashed hammock could keep one afloat for about 12 hours, it was reckoned. We slept on the tables or lockers. At one time, destroyer personnel received "Hard-Lying" (i.e. "Hard-Living") money. This was discontinued, it was said, after Lady Astor sailed in a destroyer from Portsmouth to the Isle of Wight, on a summer's day, and declared that "Hard-Lying money" was unnecessary. She was frequently mentioned, by the crew, when we were in very severe weather conditions.

Whenever we were in harbour, there was always painting to be done. It was generally considered that the ship carried more paint than ammunition. It seemed to me that I was either painting over the side or up the mast. At Milford Haven when I was up the mast painting, I saw a whaler (i.e. a 27-foot long rowing boat, which was carried by all warships). I approached our Commander and suggested that we should form a racing whaler's crew. He asked if I had any relevant experience, and I said yes. (My brother and I had occasionally taken out a rowing boat in Rouken Glen pond.) Since we needed a lot of practice, we were all excused duties, such as painting, etc.

When we were practising at Scapa Flow one day, a Force 7 gale blew up. There were two Canadian Tribal Class Destroyers, HMCS *Iroquois* and HMCS *Algonquin*. Fortunately we were quite near them so we rowed to the nearest one (I can't remember which one) and were allowed to tie up and climb on board. They sent a signal to our ship saying that we were safe on board. After some time, it was calm enough for us to return. They loaded us up with tins of fruit and other goodies that we had not seen for a long time.

On another occasion, at Milford Haven, when we were out rowing, there was a Coastal Command Sunderland Flying Boat (NSQ) moored and someone was working on it. We rowed over and I asked him if there was any chance of a flight. He said I should speak to the Captain, who happened to be on board, so he went to get him. The Captain said they were due to go out in about an hour's time for a two-hour flight, and he would be willing to take some of us. We rowed back quickly to the ship and I asked our Commander for permission to go. He agreed, provided he could come too! So we all went and I took some photographs of, in and from, the plane. We reciprocated the following day by taking about 12 RAF personnel on a short trip in the English Channel, escorting the USS *Mount Vernon*, along with the destroyer *Serapis*. We returned to Milford Haven, after about 20 hours, to drop off the RAF men.

One of my jobs for a time was "Buoy-Jumper". When a ship came into harbour, it very often moored to a buoy. These buoys were usually cylindrical with the curved surface uppermost. There was a ring and a strip of metal, about two or three inches thick lengthwise, on either side of the ring, as foot rests for standing on the buoy. The procedure was that the motor boat took two buoy jumpers as close to the buoy as possible. They climbed on to the buoy, carrying a rope which was attached to a locking hook on a wire rope on the ship. Once the jumpers were on the buoy, the ship came as near as possible to the buoy, and let out the wire rope, so that the jumpers could pull the hook and attach it to the ring. The ship could then position itself at a safe distance from the buoy, depending on wind and sea conditions. The jumpers were then taken off the buoy by motor boat. This could be quite a dangerous operation. On one occasion, at Greenock, the other jumper and I were on the buoy for two hours, in very severe weather conditions, and the ship had great difficulty in getting close to the buoy. We were soaked and very cold, and when we were eventually taken off and back to the ship, we were each given a tot of neat rum and excused duties for the rest of the day.

In January 1945, my recommend for a commission finally came through and I went to the Royal Naval Barracks at Portsmouth for pre-commission selection. This included lecturettes, tests in Power of Command, Seamanship and Signals. We also had an Assault Course at "Whale Island", officially known as HMS *Excellent*, a Gunnery School, which had a fearsome reputation for discipline. Walking was forbidden and everything had to be done at the double. Anyone seen walking was immediately put on a charge.

Having passed this I went to HMS *Raleigh* at Plymouth for a more intensive pre-Commission Course, which lasted about a week. This included Acuity Tests, Leadership Tests, a Selective Obstacle Course and giving Lecturettes.

The war in Europe seemed to be coming to an end, and when a notice appeared about volunteers for the Far East, I put my name down. I had always wanted to travel, and the Far East, in particular, sounded interesting and attractive.

Shortly afterwards I joined a sloop, HMS *Alacrity* at Dumbarton, where she was built at Denny's Yard. A Sloop was a small anti-submarine convoy escort vessel. We did our running-in trials in the

Scottish Western Isles. At Mull, there were about 6 or 7 ships and we had an inter-ship walking race, 10 miles, from Tobermory to Salen. I came in second, wearing out a pair of boots in the process! We were taken back to Tobermory in the yacht *Philante*, which had once belonged to a German general (von Ludendorff, I think). In the Atlantic we made contact with a U-Boat (U 764) and depth-charged it until it came to the surface. With our guns trained on it, we escorted it up to Loch Eriboll in the north of Scotland. In fact, our guns could not be elevated at the time, and so were virtually useless. This was the first time we actually knew the result. We had depth-charged many U-Boats, but on some occasions although there was an oil-slick, this did not necessarily mean that they were sunk.

On our way out to the Far East, we stopped at Malta and Alexandria, Egypt. My brother was in the army, stationed in the Sudan. I wrote to him that I expected to be in Alexandria at some particular time. (It had to be written in "code", as names and places were strictly censored.) He got a flight up from Khartoum in an RAF plane, and as they approached Alexandria he saw my ship just leaving.

Once during "Captain's Round" our Commanding Officer came into our mess when I was teaching three messmates simple arithmetic and algebra, and he asked me what I was doing. I explained to him and a short time later he asked me if I would act as "Schoolmaster". On big ships there was usually an "Education Officer" from the Naval Instructor Branch, but ours was a small ship so we did not have one. I agreed, provided I was not confined to a single watch. One watch always remained on board while the others went ashore. Consequently I was given a job in the stores and my action station (previously at the guns or depth charges) was in the wheel house, as I was regarded as being a competent helmsman. In action, the cox'n took the helm, but there was very often a stand-by in case he was injured. Big ships generally had three watches whereas small ships usually had two. Not being assigned to any watch meant I could go ashore any time we were in port.

Leaving Alexandria, we went through the Suez Canal to Colombo (Ceylon), Port Darwin in Northern Australia, Morotai (Molucca Islands), Hong Kong and Shanghai. The first two British ships in Shanghai were the Sloops HMS *Redpole* and HMS *Alacrity*. There was also the American Cruiser USS *St Paul*. Three or four of the American crew failed to return to the ship after shore leave, and a notice was posted on our ship about the effects of wood alcohol, which apparently had been the cause of the Americans' disappearance. I was the first ashore and was met by two Chinese, a young man and a young woman. They had been educated at Fuchow (or Soochow) University and both spoke English. Their main purpose was to show visitors the better parts of Shanghai, and to show them good class shops where they could buy genuine articles at reasonable prices (e.g. silks were popular). They also took me to the Sun Sun Hotel for a meal, which consisted of about ten courses. After each course, a waitress handed out a hot damp cloth for hands and face, and collected them before the next course. This hotel also had a large barber shop, where all the barbers wore surgical face masks. It was one of the large (if not the largest) hotels in Shanghai. At that time, excluding the Americas, Shanghai reportedly had the tallest buildings in the world. I bought a little book entitled *Chinese Self-Taught* or something similar, written by a Missionary Minister and published about 1900. One of the so-called useful words and phrases was "My concubine has a sick head this morning". Shanghai, at that time was still an International Settlement, and there were a number of different quarters. I have walked through the British, French, German and Indian sectors, and each one had shops, restaurants, languages and police, etc., to all intents and purposes, just like the parent country. On my return to the ship, I gave a couple of short talks about Shanghai. Shortly afterwards we had a tea party on board for a number of British women who had been interned there. For some time we alternated between Hong Kong (Canton River patrol) and Shanghai (Yangtse patrol).

Later on, when there were a number of ships in Shanghai, I attended, and took part in, a Current Affairs Seminar, with Lectures and Discussions, on the Cruiser HMS *Belfast*. I was the only uncommissioned (as distinct from "non-commissioned", which includes Petty Officers, Chief Petty Officers and Warrant Officers) "Schoolmaster" there, all the others being certificated Education Officers.

One of the problems in China was currency. In Shanghai alone, there were at least four different currencies at the time. There was CRB (Chinese Reserve Bank), which had an exchange rate of something like 100,000 Yuan (Chinese Dollars) to the pound. This was introduced by the Japanese, I was told. There was CNC (Chinese National Currency) which was about 4000 Yuan to the pound. These were the two currencies I used, but there was also FNC (Federal National Currency), and the Chungking Dollar—I don't know what these rates of exchange were. (Chungking was the Central Capital, Peking the Northern Capital, and Nanking the Southern Capital.) Hong Kong had its own currency, the Hong Kong Dollar, worth at that time about 1/3d (one shilling and three pence, now about 6p). The Chinese were experts with the abacus, and could change from one currency to another in just a few seconds.

In Hong Kong Island (as distinct from Hong Kong, which included the Island, Kowloon and the New Territories, altogether over 200 islands), the capital was Victoria. My favourite haunts were the Peak, almost 3000 feet, on top of which was a structure generally known as the Japanese Memorial, and Tiger Balm Gardens. Tiger Balm was a potion, regarded throughout the Far East at that time as a panacea. There was a magnificent mansion there, belonging to the brothers Aw Boon Haw and Aw Boon Par who were millionaires and founders of the Balm. I was lucky to have been allowed into the mansion, which had an abundance of ivory, antiques and precious stones.

We also went to Hongai (Vietnam, formerly French Indo-China ex Annam), where there was the second Annamite Rebellion, and then Subic Bay (US base in the Philippines), Japan (Yokohama and Tokyo) and Sydney (Australia). Towards the end of February, we arrived in Auckland, New Zealand, where I was due for a week's leave. Many New Zealanders had generously offered their hospitality for this purpose.

From Auckland Railway Station, I took the Rotorua train to Hamilton, which took about 3 hours. I then took a bus to Cambridge where I was met by a Mrs Hyde, who drove me to her neighbour's farm at Hora Hora, about 14 miles from Cambridge. This farm belonged to Mr & Mrs Judd. Mr Judd, an Englishman, was in the British Army during the First World War. After the war, he emigrated to New Zealand. He built the farmhouse himself, and, as apparently was very common in Australia and New Zealand, there was an outside dry toilet. This was a small wooden structure on top of a hillock about 100 yards or so from the house. There was no light, and a plank with a hole in it was supported at its ends on wooden blocks. Under the plank was a drop of about 20 or 30 feet. This structure was called a "Dunny".

Mrs Judd was the daughter of Missionaries in the South Sea Islands. In the hall, there was a small but fine collection of native spears and shields from Polynesia (Melanesia or Micronesia, I can't remember which). The Judds had a son and a daughter. The daughter was a schoolteacher in one of the nearby towns. The son was slightly mentally retarded, but he was very good with animals. Whenever he stepped out of the house, he was always followed by a little lamb, which he had raised from birth when its mother died.

Breakfast was usually porridge and meat. The porridge was a solid block, kept in a wooden drawer, and Mr Judd would cut slices and pass one round to each person.

He took me to the nearby towns of Tirau and Putaruru where we visited a milk processing factory and a butter factory. The neighbour, Mr Phil Hyde, took me to Rotorua, south west of Lake Rotorua (also known as Crater Lake), where there were hot springs, spouting geysers and boiling mud pools. The air was very warm and there was an almost overpowering smell of sulphur.

We also visited Fairy Springs, where the fish could be hand fed. They would swim by and take food from one's fingers or from the palm of one's hand. On the road back, Mr Hyde stopped at a small manhole, lifted the cover off, took a kettle of water from the car, and boiled the water on the issuing steam. Further on, we stopped at the Arapurui Dam, and I was shown round the Hora Hora Power Station, and so back to base.

I did help a little with the sowing and milking, and also did some horse-riding. All in all, it was an interesting and most enjoyable week.

Back on board *Alacrity*, I wrote to Mr & Mrs Judd and Mr & Mrs Hyde to thank them for their hospitality.

After leave, I returned to Auckland. As I was due for demob, I took passage on HMS *Amethyst*, a sister ship of *Alacrity*, which was involved in the Yangtse Incident, and received a lot of publicity at the time. At Sydney I went on board the USS *Georgetown Victory*, which, we were told, would take us to Falmouth. We stopped at Fremantle, the port of Perth in Western Australia. We were allowed ashore and I went to Perth for a quick look round. Our next stops were at Colombo and Aden.

After 35 days at sea, at midnight on the 30th April/1st May 1946, there was a tremendous crash and it felt as if the ship was going upstairs and we were all thrown out of our bunks. I ran on to the upper deck and, looking over the side, could see what looked like grass. There was an announcement to say that there was no immediate danger, and that we should stay on board until the tide came in, when we would be taken ashore. What had happened was that the ship had run aground at Killard Point in Northern Ireland, although it was a very clear night and there was night flying from Bishopscourt airfield nearby. The food on board, for the passengers, was appalling. We had tomato juice and spaghetti almost every day, usually with a slice of bread with cheese and jam, while the American crew had proper meals, as we saw some of the crew carry chickens and meats across the deck. There was a "bakery", which was really a food store, and was guarded by a Royal Marine. When all the lights went out, two shipmates and I broke into the bakery and took what we could find, by touch. This consisted of a packet of corn flakes and a loaf of bread.

In the morning, when the tide had come in, we had to climb down the side of the ship with our cases on our backs, into a small boat with an American sailor at the tiller, to take us a few yards to the land. Our kit bags were in the hold and were all lost. There were about 1200 passengers (mainly seamen, going home to be demobbed) and a fleet of army trucks took us to Belfast, where we had a meal. We were then taken to the port, where we embarked on a landing craft, LCSC *Princess Iris* (Landing Craft Stern Chute) and taken to Glasgow, where a special train was to take us to the three Naval Bases (Portsmouth, Chatham and Devonport). As the train had not yet arrived, I managed to get a taxi, went home, left my case, and straight back to King George V Dock, and got there just when the train arrived. On arrival at Portsmouth (my base), we were re-kitted and then back home for 14 days survivor's leave.

On arriving back at Portsmouth, I was told that I was to take part in the Victory Parade in London on the 8th June. We practised marching for a few days and then went to Kensington Gardens, in London, where we lived in tents. At the actual parade I was in the Naval Contingent which was leading the British forces.

After that I was eventually demobbed. Sometime later I received an official photograph of the Naval Contingent in the parade. There was a single Officer immediately in front of the Contingent. It so happened that he had been my Commanding Officer on the *Nubian*. A few years later I visited my brother in Belfast and we went to Killard Point. The ship was still there, its back broken into three pieces. Sometime later the press reported that there was a Court Martial. The Captain had been drunk (it was his last voyage, in more ways than one!) and I think he was dismissed with ignominy.

I was lucky to get some photographs of the stranded ship from the press, from the Irish papers (from my brother, Wolfe Sacharin O.B.E., F.R.I.C.S., Director of Building Services N.I.) and a lot of information from the National Maritime Museum in London, and in one of the photographs I am shown stepping into the small boat.

Interestingly, and by a strange coincidence, all my Commanding Officers had double-barrelled names:

Captain Otway-Ruthven RN (Force J2)
Lt. Commander Pack-Beresford RN (HMS *Nubian*)
Lt. Commander Clutton-Baker RNR (HMS *Alacrity*)

The War was tragic and horrendous and millions were killed, wounded and bereaved. I was one of the lucky ones, having travelled widely and visited places that I would never otherwise have seen. I did have my hearing quite severely damaged and this was recognised by the War Pensions Directorate of the Department of Social Security. As a result of this I received a War Disablement Pension (actually a Gratuity, i.e. a single lump sum payment). However, compared to others, I was extremely fortunate.


**Return to Civilian Life**

I was demobbed in June 1946. I went back to University, starting the course from the beginning and again working in various shipyards (one at a time). My father had Pulmonary Tuberculosis and every winter was confined to bed. Anti-Tubercle drugs were not available and his condition deteriorated. We were always short of money, and after two years at University I took time off for two years to finish my apprenticeship and to earn more money to pay my fees.

The Engineering Course was an Honours Course and was also a group degree. There were seven subjects to be passed at the one sitting. Failure in one subject generally meant failure in them all, unless there were special circumstances. Thus one could be referred in at most two subjects, provided that good passes were obtained in the remaining five. In addition, one had to pass a Subsidiary Subject and at least one Additional Subject. The Subsidiary Subject was specified, but there was a very wide choice of Additional Subjects. I took four (the maximum allowed): Economics, Aeroneutics, Industrial Psychology and Advanced Mathematics.

My father died three weeks before my Final Examinations. By this time all my brothers and sisters were married and I was the only one at home to support my mother. A few weeks later my mother fell, damaging the base of her spine and she was hospitalised. Needless to say, I failed the group examinations. At Glasgow University, one can sit only once for Honours. While I do not know what the rules are in other Scottish Universities, in English Universities one can re-sit any number of times. In fact, it is possible to re-sit examinations to improve the class of Honours.

I re-sat my examinations in September and was referred in two subjects in the group. I passed all the others. I re-sat in March and passed the one. The Syllabus for the other course had been changed and I knew nothing about it. I was advised to re-attend in this particular subject, but could not afford to.

I wrote to the Senate, explaining the position. They said they would set a special examination paper, based on the Course I had taken, and if successful they would award, not a degree, but a Certificate of Proficiency in Engineering (C.P.E.). This seemed to be quite popular with foreign (mainly Scandinavian) students. Although I had passed all the examinations I did not graduate with a BSc but with the aforementioned Certificate.

Students were encouraged to take part in extracurricular activities and I was advised to join the boxing club. I was the Captain of the Boxing Club for two years.

After leaving the University I worked as a Naval Architect in various shipyards. By 1954, I felt that Shipbuilding on the Clyde was declining and that there was no future there for me. Since I had studied Aerodynamics, I wrote to Scottish Aviation at Prestwick to find out if any work was available for me. I went for an interview and could have had a job there as an Aerodynamicist. However, although I would have liked to work there, the money was not sufficient for me to change, so I declined. A year later, I received a letter from the Director saying that they were now in a position to offer me more money. So I became an Aerodynamicist, latterly in a senior position.

In 1957 I went on Tropical Trials to Aden and High Altitude Trials in Ethiopia (Eritrea). My mother's health began to deteriorate. She developed Glaucoma and she began to suffer from tuberculosis again. In 1958 she died from a pulmonary haemorrhage. She must have got up during the night and collapsed. If she called me, I did not hear her, but when I got up in the morning I found her lying in the kitchen (she slept in the recess in the kitchen). I was shattered by the experience.

Early in 1959 I met Rosa and we gradually got to know each other. We found we had a great deal in common. However, in March of that year, after a short courtship, I again went on Tropical Trials, this time to Libya, and High Altitude Trials in Switzerland. On return we continued to see each other and decided to marry on the 29th December 1959.

# Chapter 18

## Marriage and Motherhood

After a short courtship we decided to get married. We were both mature enough to recognize the problems marriage could bring but felt we could deal with these. The marriage took place on the 29$^{th}$ December 1959 in Langside Synagogue and the Reception and Dinner were held in the Grand Hotel, Charing Cross.

We made our home in Joe's flat in Pollokshaws Road, Glasgow, and intended to find a house more suited to our needs.

On the whole we found it easy to adjust to married life. We had mutual respect for one another and were willing to make allowances for each of our different personality traits. My family seemed to have greater difficulty in adjusting to my changing status and the relationship between us was strained at times. While I had been always available to my family with help when help was needed, my first consideration had to be my husband and his needs. There seemed to be a feeling of animosity towards Joe, which was already apparent before my marriage. While I had relatively little difficulty in keeping my distance from Joe's sisters in particular, I found it more difficult to distance myself from my sister. Betty had her own problems and I was always there to give support. It was only to be expected that that support, which, while still possible, had to be more limited.

Joe was very close to his family and seemed to me to be under their influence. This also caused some tension. However, I never attempted to loosen the bond he felt for his family and made a point of sharing our contact with both sides.

I continued to work at Yorkhill. Joe was working at Prestwick, but he thought that the future prospects there were limited. He decided to go into Further Education teaching mathematics and statistics. His first College was in Coatbridge, moving later to Stow College in Glasgow where he eventually retired as Senior Lecturer. Joe enjoyed teaching and was not keen on administration and therefore made no effort to apply for such a post. He had a good working relationship with his colleagues with whom we also had social contacts.

In 1960 we bought a terraced house in Vennard Gardens, which was just around the corner of the flat we lived in.

I was much more ambitious. I had felt for many years that there were no suitable books available dealing with Paediatric nursing. I decided to write a book specifically on Paediatric Nursing Procedures. The idea was to highlight the essential differences when caring for children compared to adults. The more I became involved in writing this book, the more I realised my limitations. I was more orientated towards Medical Nursing, though I did have a good grounding in Surgical Nursing. I decided to ask Peggy Hunter, who was a clinical teacher at Yorkhill and more involved with Surgical Nursing, to join me in that project. She was very enthusiastic and supportive. Since the idea was mine I suggested to her that we have equal share in the Royalties. She agreed.

I became pregnant in 1961 and continued to work until the seventh month of pregnancy when it was compulsory to cease work. Carole was born on the 7th November 1961. It was not an easy labour and she had to be delivered by forceps. She was a lovely baby. Unfortunately I was unable to breast-feed and that made me feel unhappy. However, she thrived well. I had a home-help to begin with but before long was able to establish a routine which was suitable for her and ourselves. I was often anxious and being aware of the problems, which could arise, perhaps increased my anxiety. I was perhaps overprotective in that I was frightened that she might be infected. Carole progressed well and she responded readily to both of us. Her progress was satisfactory in all areas of development and I kept a careful record. It is so easy to forget what a baby/child achieved at various stages, that it was important to record everything.

During that time I continued to write the book *Paediatric Nursing Procedures* which was published in 1964. By that time I was pregnant again and our second daughter was born on the 24th September 1964. Dr Armstrong, my first obstetrician, had died and I was cared for by his successor. After my first labour I had been told that a caesarean section would be safer in my case. By the time of my second pregnancy I was 39 years old and since my uterus did not function effectively with the first labour I had hoped that he would consider that. However, he thought I should deliver normally. Unfortunately I had the same difficulty and the baby had to be delivered by forceps. While I had a general anaesthetic for Carole's delivery, for Marion's, I was given a Pudendal Block. The purpose of this local anaesthetic is to eliminate the pain of Forceps delivery whilst the mother remains fully conscious and, at the same time, the baby is not affected by the local anaesthetic. While I did not experience pain, the sensation of the pull on the head of the baby was dreadful. Marion cried immediately after being born, but the sensations of this type of delivery created nightmares for me for many months after the delivery.

Like Carole, Marion was easy to care for. Both babies settled in well and by the third month, slept all night. Her progress was very good and Carole responded lovingly to her new sister.

When Carole was three years old I noticed a swelling on her neck line. This was diagnosed as a lipoma and was removed at Yorkhill when she was four years old. Mr Bentley was a good surgeon and the incision he made was along the neck line and left no mark or at least could be hidden by a necklace.

Both children were able to read by the age of three and showed understanding of the concept of numbers. They had little problems with schoolwork.

Carole was a timid child and had difficulty in standing her ground with other children. At an early age she exhibited an inability to withstand bullies. She made few friends, particularly while at primary school where she was often intimidated. I rarely saw her school jotter until it was full and unless there were problems, there was little contact with the teachers until she brought home the jotter. This particular jotter showed that her work was good until I read the last page, when Carole wrote a short essay ending that the school was "like a concentration camp". The teacher was obviously angry or upset and she made her opinion known with a comment in red where she chided Carole, and wrote that she would not tolerate such a comment. I was quite shattered and asked Carole what the problem was. She was obviously very unhappy and I felt that I really must discuss this issue with the teacher. I therefore went to the school and asked the Headmaster's permission to speak to the teacher. He asked if he could be present and I agreed. The teacher was young and this was her first teaching post. It was a very useful discussion we had and I explained to the teacher that she had missed a good learning opportunity herself. In not recognising that here was a very unhappy child and instead of being angry and hurt, she should have attempted to find out what the problem was and perhaps contacted me. I was very much aware of the bullying element amongst children and it was important that the teachers understood that they have a responsibility in protecting the vulnerable children while in their care.

It was a very useful discussion; there was no aggression on my part and both the Head teacher and the young teacher felt that it was a useful exercise.

When Marion was three months old I thought that her hearing was defective. She was given the Griffith's test and although she responded, she was to be retested at 6 months of age. At this time the test proved satisfactory. However, I still felt that there was a problem somewhere. By the time she was three years old Marion was able to recognise letters and showed good understanding of the concept of numbers. One day when waiting to cross the road, a pigeon landed near her and she was very frightened. She did not see it coming. At that time she could read already. I tested her vision, but not distance vision. I was somewhat concerned.

She started school, and on the first day, when I collected her she cried and told me that she could not see the blackboard. I went straight back into the classroom and spoke to the teacher, who thought it was the sunshine which might have caused her problems. I tested her there and then and, indeed, Marion proved to be short-sighted. This was confirmed at Yorkhill where she was diagnosed as a high myopic. I was shattered. She was given glasses and the first time we went for a drive along the Greenock road, Marion called the buoys "ships". She had never seen far away objects clearly. She accepted wearing glasses and her progress continued very satisfactorily. She was a bright little girl, made friends easily and formed a particular friendship with Fiona.

I was very fond of music and as a child wanted to learn to play the violin. I had bought a violin in Israel but did not continue to take lessons when I returned to Glasgow. Since I could play the piano in a very elementary way, we bought a piano and I enjoyed playing it in my amateurish way. Carole seemed interested in the piano and asked to have lessons. When she was six she was enrolled at Langside College, which was near enough and she was introduced to piano playing, going on a Saturday morning for lessons. She made good progress and showed promise. When her piano teacher died we did not know who to go to.

It was the practice in primary school for young children to write a short piece of prose in their day book, a type of diary. Carole was obviously anxious about continuing her piano lessons and wrote into her book that she now did not have a teacher. Mrs Dunworth, her teacher at Shawlands Primary School, read her entry and suggested to her that she might be able to help. I telephoned her and since she indicated that although she was not qualified to teach piano, she had studied the piano to grade 8 (which is the highest grade available before more advanced study of the piano). We agreed that she should teach Carole at home. Mrs Dunworth had a gentle touch and proved to be excellent for Carole. It was interesting to see that Carole was able to differentiate the two roles of Mrs Dunworth and as Mrs Dunworth indicated, Carole was a different person when she taught her at home. While she was quiet and shy in class, she was a real chatterbox with her at home. Carole made good progress, sat and passed her piano examinations.

The point came when Mrs Dunworth felt that Carole required more advanced piano tuition and that she was not qualified to do so. Meanwhile, Marion had become very friendly with Fiona whose mother was a concert pianist and also taught piano. I asked her mother if she would take Carole as a pupil, which she agreed to do. The standard of playing and tuition was on a very high level. While Mrs Dunworth had a gentle approach to playing the piano, Sheila was a very accomplished pianist whose playing was much more forceful. Carole was ready for such an approach and again made good progress. I was early on aware that Carole did not have the temperament to play in front of other people; however, I felt it to be important that she should be competent in playing the piano.

Marion was not interested in playing the piano but wanted to play the violin. She started her lessons with Mr Graham, a peripatetic teacher of violin. He was enthusiastic and taught the children as a group. I engaged him to teach Marion privately, since her progress in the group setting was very slow. Marion argued a great deal with him and he was too gentle to enforce an element of discipline.

By that time Fiona was progressing by leaps and bounds in her violin playing. She had of course the great advantage of a mother who was a trained and very competent musician, while I could not provide the expertise both Carole and Marion needed.

We attended a concert given by children who were taught the violin by Mr Jacobs. All the children played from memory and the standard was very high. When Mr Graham left, I approached Mr Jacobs and he agreed to teach Marion. I think the change to his method was quite a shock to Marion and at times she seemed quite stressed. He made great demands and was slow to praise. However, Marion began to make good progress and although she was technically not as good as Fiona, she showed feeling for the music she played.

Sheila MacLean was also employed as a peripatetic music teacher and she was very active in the musical field. She had her own trio, known as the "Lessel's trio" (the name Lessel was her maiden name). While attending one of the trio's performances, Carole was moved to tears by the cellist's playing of Bruch's "Kol Niddre". She expressed the wish to learn to play the cello. Sheila suggested that we ask Miss Dick, a cello teacher, to teach Carole, which she gladly did. Carole made good progress learning to play the cello and had no difficulty learning both instruments. She always complained that she did not have an accompanist. My piano playing was totally inadequate to meet her or Marion's needs. Marion, however, had Carole to accompany her violin playing. To encourage both girls, we asked them to play at various venues, none of them too demanding, i.e. Blind Society. Neither of them were keen to do so and I thought that to be a great pity. While I realised that Marion did not have the discipline or patience, and perhaps was also not all that interested in playing an instrument, Carole was much more eager to do well, but did not have performer stamina or temperament. With Sheila's guidance she was encouraged to teach piano playing to young children and was given one or two children to teach. She had a good rapport with them and was able to teach them for some time until she got married and left for America.

At least Carole did complete her initial training in piano to Grade 8 and cello to Grade 6, while Marion did not sit any violin examination. This was partly due to Mr Jacobs' resistance to prepare his pupils for these tests. When Mr Jacobs became a Lecturer at the Royal Academy for Music and Drama in Glasgow, he ceased to teach Marion. We found another teacher for her. Her approach was more conventional and she and Marion worked well together. I felt Marion was happier with her, but also knew that she would not continue beyond that level.

Both girls coped well with their schoolwork. Marion became dux of the Primary School. Both went to Shawlands Academy, being placed in the A-Stream. Marion showed early on a good understanding of mathematical concepts and Carole understood reasonably well. They did not cope well with Physics and Chemistry and since they wanted to study medicine, they had to obtain high grades in these subjects.

We felt that Carole should concentrate on art subjects including music, but she was totally against it. I think she felt that we wanted her to become a performer, but this was not the case. We thought that she was good at music and could have gained a teaching qualification in that field.

As far as Marion was concerned, we also felt that she was not suited temperamentally to medicine and should concentrate on mathematics. Neither girls were amenable to advice and discussions about careers often led to arguments. Although both obtained reasonably good grades in their Highers, we felt that both could have done better.

Carole's grades were not good enough for admission to Glasgow University for medicine and she was not keen to do a sixth year at Shawlands. She eventually was admitted to Glasgow College where she studied applied Biology. She did well in the first year but in the third year had difficulty and had to re-sit one of the examinations. She passed on re-sitting it and obtained a BSc in 1982.

Since our holidays to America in 1977 Carole had been corresponding with Allan. The relationship blossomed and she visited him in 1981. After only one visit, they decided to become engaged, intending to get married in 1983. Alan was 11 months younger than Carole and still a student, studying Computer Science and Mathematics. We were rather concerned and advised them to wait until Alan had finished his studies and had some means of earning money. Alan's parents did not see anything wrong in their son's decision, so we got no support for our view.

Alan visited us in December 1982. We still felt that he was too young for such a responsibility, but both of them were very keen and plans were made for their wedding in June 1983. Herb, Gloria (Alan's parents) and Ben, his brother came for the wedding as well as three other relatives of Alan's. The rest of the guests were from our side. It was a happy occasion, but I still had niggling doubts.

137

Carole had applied for a visa but due to inefficiency at the Consulate, this was not ready. They were due to leave for the US in a fortnight's time. Herb travelled to London with Carole and Alan and eventually everything was ready for them to travel. Carole and Alan were to stay with Herb and Gloria (not a good arrangement) but since Alan was still at University, they had no means of paying for a home of their own. Joe and I were very worried.

Meanwhile Marion completed her education at Langside College, obtaining further passes at A-level and was accepted at Aberdeen University to study Mathematics and Computer Science. Marion was very keen to leave home and did not apply to Glasgow University.

We took her to Aberdeen and saw her settled in at the Campus. She seemed happy and hoped that she would cope. Her approach to University life was more positive than Carole's had been and she took an active part in various extra-curricular activities i.e. operatic society. We made sure that she had enough money at all times and gave her an allowance, apart from the student grant she received from the State. Marion kept in touch with us; indeed she phoned us often and required a great deal of reassurance. In her second year she moved out of the student accommodation to live in the Hillel House. This was a flat in the Synagogue, which she shared with another student. Eventually Richard moved into the flat and they seemed to get on well together. Richard studied art and design and was a gifted student.

Marion exhibited signs of depression and required a great deal of support and reassurance. At the end of the second year she wanted to have a year out to travel. We were very much against it and told her so. Fortunately she accepted our advice and continued at Aberdeen University, completing her course and obtaining her BSc in 1984.

Marion decided to buy a flat and Richard shared it with her. We paid the deposit for the flat. Since she could not get work as programmer, she obtained a post as office worker in a company called Oceangraphic. They did programming for oil exploration work. She eventually was asked to join the programming team.

Marion became restless and decided to move on. She applied and was accepted as programmer with Cadbury-Schweppes and to begin with enjoyed the work. After a year she decided to move on and we had to pay the transfer money she owed Cadbury-Schweppes. She bought a flat in London, letting the flat in Aberdeen. We also paid the deposit for that flat. She changed employment twice; the last time we did not know what happened to her since she stopped communicating with us. Eventually she told us that she had moved to Birmingham and had formed her own company (Hillbrent Computers Ltd with Mick as Partner). Mick was working with Cadbury-Schweppes and they formed a relationship, which seemed to be quite a close one. Mick was not Jewish and we were rather unhappy about that but had and have accepted that.

Contact with Marion became less frequent and when her cousin Sylvia indicated that she was visiting Marion, I mentioned it to her, warning her that she needs to be careful what she says to Sylvia, since a number of statements emanating from her had reached us. I am afraid that led to a rift between Marion and us. In fact, she wrote a letter accusing us of not caring for her or supporting her, that we lacked understanding of her problems. Some of the accusations and statements in the letter required a full response and we answered all the points she made. We tried hard to heal the rift and visited her on three occasions. She made no effort to contact us or inquire how we were getting on. We met Mick on three occasions and liked him as a person. In fact the third time we simply arrived at her house. While she was upset at seeing us, she eventually calmed down and seemed warm towards us. We parted then on friendly terms.

Marion told us that she was going to the Bahamas for her holidays. We heard nothing from her. We wrote to her and received a letter with photographs from her, telling us that she and Mick were married in Fiji. While we were very upset, we were not totally surprised. What upset us even more was her statement that she did not wish to have anything to do with us. It is not easy to describe our feelings at her rejection of us, but we decided to respect her wishes to keep out of her life. There has been no contact between us since July 1996, though we sent her birthday cards.

# Chapter 19

## Need for Intellectual Stimuli

While the children were young I concentrated on their care. However, even during those years I attended extra-mural classes at Glasgow University, covering subjects such as Child Psychology, Logic, Human Relations and Physiological Control Systems. I found these stimulating.

The Royal College of Nursing started a two-year part-time course in conjunction with the University in London leading to the Diploma in Nursing. I decided to apply for this course and was accepted. I started the first part in 1971.

When the Open University was established Joe became a Counsellor at the Open University. He suggested that I should apply to become a student at the Open University. I did not feel that I could undertake study at University level, but he thought otherwise.

After much persuasion, I applied for admission to the Open University and was accepted. At that time Nursing qualifications were not recognised for Foundation Course exemption and I registered for Social Science and Science Foundation Courses. I had to struggle with some aspects of the Science Course, since I did not have the basic knowledge in subjects such as mathematics, physics or chemistry. It was therefore quite hard for me but I was fortunate to pass these examinations and proceeded to other courses to complete the degree. These were second, third and fourth level courses including subjects such as Biological Basis of Behaviour, Organisation of Cells, Genetics Educational Studies and Industrial Psychology. I also had to attend Summer Schools lasting one week each. These were very demanding and at the end of these felt utterly shattered and tired. I had to work very hard doing the course work while at the same time giving support to my children and my husband, who was extremely supportive in all that I was doing. My grades were not brilliant but I managed to pass all the examinations and course work and obtained my degree of BA in 1975.

When the children were 11 and 8 years old I returned to Nursing on a part-time basis. The reason for my return was initially to fulfil the conditions of my Diploma of Nursing. The Lectures were given by Tutors appointed by the Royal College of Nursing and were held in Stobhill Hospital.

I passed the first part of the Course and required practical input to fulfil the course requirements which was based on an in-depth study of two cases. Since I opted for Sick Children's Nursing study, I applied for a post at Yorkhill thus returning to nursing, initially on a part-time basis, but soon full-time.

On my return to Yorkhill I was employed as a Clinical Teacher, attending the lectures on one day a week. One case was a two-year-old boy suffering from Nephrotic Syndrome and the other one a two-year-old child diagnosed as "Failure to Thrive".

Of the two cases, the second one was the more difficult one and involved not only the nursing management of the child, but also study of the behaviour and attitude of the mother towards her child and the effect these had on the child. The first case required a more academic approach, showing understanding of the patho-physiological basis of the condition, its effect on the child and the management of care. The oral examination seemed to concentrate on the case Failure to thrive and was thorough and covered many aspects of Growth and Development as well as management of nursing care and Child Psychology. I passed the second part of the course and obtained a Diploma in Nursing (Paediatric Nursing) from London University.

When Jordanhill College of Further Education started a course for Nurse Teachers, I applied and was accepted. This was an in-service course consisting of Blocks of Theory of Education and Learning and practical teaching in two Nurse Training Colleges. I passed the examinations and became a Registered Nurse Teacher in 1975.

When all these courses were successfully completed the family celebrated with a dinner in a hotel. I was somewhat taken aback when Marion said: "It is nice to have you back." I had really tried hard to be there for my children and only asked for time to study as from 8 p.m. to do the necessary course work.

It brought me back down to earth and I felt guilty that perhaps in my need and endeavour to feed my craving for intellectual satisfaction, I perhaps failed to be "there for my children". I had always been there for them and supported them in all that they were doing and only asked to be allowed to study from 8 p.m. when their day's activities were completed.

I continued working in Yorkhill as a Nurse Teacher and decided to write a book on Paediatric Nursing. This book was to be a textbook and would include Anatomy and Physiology as applied to children, Pathological states and Nursing care. I found an excellent illustrator to provide the illustrations for the text and photographs, etc., to enhance the text. The book, *Principles of Paediatric Nursing*, was published in 1980. A second edition was published in 1986 with translations in Spanish and Indonesian Bahasa.

In 1981 I received a letter informing me that I had been nominated in the competition in the *Sunday Mail* "Scottish Nurse of the Year 1981" award. I did not and do not know who put my name forward. On the day of the competition it was felt that I did not really fit into the category of "bedside" nurse since I was a tutor. I was therefore given a special award in the form of an engraved plate which said "For Outstanding Service to Nursing". It was of course a great honour and I felt very touched by this award. However, I do feel that such competitions are extremely difficult to judge and it is not really possible to make a judgement which is fair to all.

*Presentation of engraved plate (from "Nurse of the Year" programme)*

I was quite frustrated at times. The standard of teaching was not very good and the level of knowledge quite low. There was no chance of advancement at Yorkhill and I was keen to remain in Paediatrics. There was a move to amalgamate the individual training schools into Colleges of Nursing and there was a danger that Paediatric Nurse training would be absorbed into the general field. The present set up was not economical. Smaller Training schools were seeking amalgamation with larger ones like Yorkhill. One example was Ayrshire which was seeking to amalgamate its Paediatric Course with Yorkhill. Those in Charge at the Yorkhill Training School were not keen, but I thought it was a good idea. When the post for Senior Tutor was advertised for Ayrshire, I applied.

The year was 1981 when I went for an interview at Crosshouse Hospital, which also housed the Ayrshire and Arran College of Nursing. The interview went well. I was offered the post as Senior Tutor in Paediatric nursing and I accepted it. I only had another four years before I was due to retire and this was an opportunity to reach that level and for the first time use my ideas for the Sick Children's Nursing Course.

## Move to the Ayrshire and Arran College of Nursing and Midwifery

There were only a few nurses taking the course. The level of experience was very limited. Latterly they had been taught by Tutors who had neither Paediatric knowledge nor experience, and they were pretty disillusioned with nursing. There was also no liaison between the College and Service.

My first task was to look at the course structure and reorganise the programme. While the College was situated in Kilmarnock, the Sick Children's' Hospital was in Ayr. The building housing the hospital was an interesting one, but totally unsuitable for a hospital. Although some modern equipment was available, many of the basic ones were of poor quality, e.g. bath thermometers. A new hospital was waiting completion and this was to contain a children's unit. I had to orientate myself to the area and the community. While obviously there was little scope for wide-reaching changes, there were a number of areas where improvements were vital. As part of my orientation, I went to the Scottish Home and Health Department and spoke to the Chief Nursing Officer. I therefore got a wider view of the issues and possibilities.

Apart from having responsibility for nurses preparing for registration I was also involved with the community programme for all nurses taking the adult general and psychiatric nursing courses. This involved organising the theoretical part of the course and placement in areas such as community, children's nursing for general and psychiatric students and midwifery for all students.

Since I had no other tutors to help me, I also had to ensure that there was a proper group structure. For that purpose, I had to persuade qualified Sick Children's Nurses with good experience to become clinical teachers and teachers. There was some opposition from the College Director and with the appointment of a new Chief Area Nursing Officer, I soon became aware that the higher echelons were not interested in continuing the Sick Children's Nursing Course.

A new programme of training was due to start and I was able to introduce some of my ideas. There were limitations because of the limited areas of practical experience. For example, there was no intensive care unit for children, and any specialist treatment required transfer to Yorkhill in Glasgow. The amount of money available was also limited. However, I managed to include experience for nurses in child psychiatry, though mainly in a clinic i.e. out-patient setting. We visited areas of interest i.e. Hansel Village, which caters for people with learning difficulties (mentally handicapped) and also visited Day nurseries. I also obtained permission to send senior nurses to the neonatal unit in Yorkhill for experience in intensive care nursing. I felt that this was very important, because Ayrshire had no facilities for treating new-born babies with severe abnormalities.

As part of my remit as Senior Tutor (Community Nursing) I held teaching sessions for Health Visitors, Community Nurses and School Nurses. Since these groups of nurses gave support to parents and their children in the community, it was important that they should have some basic knowledge of the problems of the sick child and how to deal with them. I was also involved in establishing a community nursing service relevant to sick children, being cared for at home. This service was managed by nurses with the requisite qualification and experience.

In 1984 the Ayrshire and Aran Health Board decided to discontinue the Sick Children's Nursing Course. I was very upset and organised a protest against the decision. I wrote to the then Secretary of State for Scotland and hoped to get the support of the local MP. While the Secretary of State was sympathetic (he was an Ayrshire MP), the local MP was not. The acting CANO and the Director were upset at my action and I was called to a disciplinary hearing. Despite having been given an assurance that I could remain in post until the completion of the course, when my retiral date came, I was not asked to stay on. Fortunately by that time I had two trained tutors who would supervise the training until the nurses sat their final examination.

Just before I was due to retire on the 23rd March 1985, I was asked if I would like to take up a teaching post at Kilmarnock College to teach Medical Secretaries. The subjects included basic anatomy and physiology, with the emphasis on Medical terminology, since as secretaries some knowledge of the words used and their meaning was an important part of their work. I accepted, and it was agreed that I should start teaching at Kilmarnock College after the Easter Holidays.

# Chapter 20

## My Mother's Health Deteriorates

My mother's condition continued to deteriorate. She was not eating and was losing weight. Eventually she was diagnosed as having a duodenal ulcer, which was bleeding. She had symptoms of it in her younger days but this time she had a severe recurrence. She had collapsed in the synagogue and was admitted to the Victoria Infirmary. Treatment was successful but I decided that she no longer could live on her own and therefore she moved in with us.

After Henry died, Betty decided to be near to her daughter Rose and left in February 1985 to settle in Israel. I continued to work at Crosshouse, but was anxious about my mother who was beginning to show evidence of dementia.

One day when I returned home from work, my mother was not at home. I telephoned various hospitals and notified the police. At 8 p.m. I received a telephone call from the police to the effect that they had found my mother wandering on the Kingston Bridge. This bridge spans the river Clyde and is only used for vehicles. It was a miracle she was not hit by a car.

The police brought her home. She was exhausted, hungry and bewildered. I also found that she had £400 in her pocket. She had withdrawn the money from her Building Society account. She was not aware that she had been to the Building Society and I realised that I would have to take greater control of her affairs. I spoke to the lawyer and he agreed that I should have Power of Attorney. This way I could ask the Bank and Building Society not to issue her with any money.

When I retired from Nursing at the end of March 1985, I made arrangement with the Social Work Department to have a Home Help. This was to allow me to continue to work three days a week and ensure that during these days my mother had a midday meal. My mother was not happy about the arrangement, but she accepted it.

I started work at Kilmarnock College after the Easter holidays. The Medical Secretaries Course lasted two years and I was asked to teach basic Anatomy and Physiology, primarily so that the students could understand the terms used in these sciences and know how to spell the terms. Also Medical Terminology, both the history and the meaning of words. In the second year I taught First Aid and the Laws relating to Health and Safety at Work as well as more advanced terminology. Originally I attended for three days a week, teaching every period. This was decreased to two and a half days a week. I enjoyed teaching the students and found the work satisfying.

I remained at Kilmarnock College from 1985 until 1988. During that time my mother's mental and physical state deteriorated. When my mother first came to stay with us she agitated to go to Israel and stay with Betty. Indeed, the arrangement had been that the care of my mother should be shared so that Betty would look after her for six months.

In June 1985 there was an International Nurses Conference in Israel and I took my mother with me to stay with my sister, as we had agreed. I attended the conference and on returning home Joe and I went on Holiday. Throughout her time with Betty, I heard nothing but complaints and although my mother was to stay until August, Betty sent her back earlier. She travelled on her own and I received a telephone call from Heathrow airport that my mother had arrived and that no one was with her. There was no one in London I could have asked to look after her, nor was it possible that I flew to London to collect her. The staff at the airport were helpful, put her on the plane to Glasgow and we collected her at Glasgow airport.

She settled down with us but her mental and physical state deteriorated. She now required 24-hours care. My nights were very disturbed and for three years I did not have a restful night. I arranged that someone was with her during the day, e.g. a home help and a carer from Crossroads, a voluntary organisation caring for elderly demented patients. My mother's vision also deteriorated and she had very frequent transient ischaemic attacks, some of them leading to prolonged periods of unconsciousness. These were the forerunner of major cerebral haemorrhages.

My own health was not good at that time and I required beta-blockers to deal with heart arrhythmias and it became obvious that both Joe and I could not cope with the strain. Joe, throughout my mother's stay with us, was very supportive.

She was assessed by a doctor dealing with elderly dementia patients and he advised that my mother required constant supervision and care and I reluctantly agreed to have her admitted to Newark Lodge, the Jewish Old Age Home. I felt very guilty sending my mother to a Home and, although it was the only course to take, I never failed to feel unhappy about that decision.

I was determined that her care should be the best available and had to deal with a number of complaints and discussed these with the staff. They also knew that I was willing to help and there were occasions when I was called to the home to calm and reassure my mother. I visited her 3-4 times a week and took her for walks if she was able to do so. It was also important that she was in a Jewish environment; even so, she had little awareness of what went on around her.

Her mental and physical state further deteriorated and eventually she was moved to the hospital part of the Home. She had a major cerebral haemorrhage and became unconscious and never regained consciousness. She was kept comfortable and since she developed pneumonia was given antibiotics and kept well hydrated.

I stayed with her for the last three days of her life and kept Betty informed of her deteriorating condition. Betty arrived just in time and on the 2nd December 1988, one day before her 92nd birthday, my mother died. Jetty had always been very fond of my mother, who was, in many ways, like a mother to her, and she came for her funeral. Carole and Alan made a great effort to come to the funeral and I was very grateful for their presence and support. Marion did not come to the funeral.

My mother had a very difficult life and not a happy one. However, her indomitable spirit and her faith kept her going. It helped her to survive the tremendous difficulties she experienced during the war. She was capable of much love and always willing to help. She tried hard to keep our little family together, but was not always able to do so effectively.

I was sad that, for the last two years of her life, I could not provide her with the care she needed in my home and, although it was the right decision to send her to Newark Lodge, I felt guilty for having done so. As I already stated, I made sure that her care was the best possible and was with her during her last few days and hope that she felt my love and compassion for her.

# Chapter 21

## Searching for Answers

Throughout our married life Joe and I used our holidays not just for getting away from home and change of scenery, but to see new places and learn as much as possible about the countries, cities and people we visited. While the children were young we decided to use holidays not simply to sunbathe or play but to introduce them to a world beyond their home environment. We had to take into account their age and level of understanding. While in this narrative I will concentrate on my search for answers, this did not happen until they were living their own lives. However, even when quite young they became aware of differences and problems since they were exposed to the tearful outbursts of my mother but were sheltered from the realities I will be writing about. It must have affected them and indeed Carole, in her school jotter, once compared school to a concentration camp (during one of the unhappy episodes in primary school).

In 1963 when Carole was quite young we took her to Denmark and visited Jetty. This was the first time that I stepped on German soil since 1938. Since we travelled by car we had to pass through northern Germany to get to Puttgarten. I was rather tense and apprehensive and did not know how I would cope meeting Germans. It was a little frightening since we had to pass through, what seemed to me, rather officious and threatening border controls. Many cars were stripped and searched and it was quite frightening. However, we had no problems and were allowed through the controls fairly quickly. The journey to Puttgarten was pleasant and before boarding the Ferry we spent the night at a Bed and Breakfast place in Travemünde. The next morning we boarded the Ferry, which took us to Rodbyhaven in southern Denmark.

Jetty made us most welcome in her little flat and Carole was a great hit with all who came in contact with her. Jetty's friends, Berl and Esther, made us most welcome and allowed us to stay in their lovely home while they were on holiday.


**First visit to Berlin in 1966**

In 1966 we decided to start camping for our holidays. We bought a family tent and other equipment, which we thought necessary, most of these on the advice and guidance of people, we believed, were experienced campers. We soon learned otherwise as we set off on our first camping holiday.

We decided that the main area to visit was to be Yugoslavia and since the route was through Germany our first port of call was to be Berlin to visit Tante Anna, who had been a loving, caring person to me since 1929.

It might be interesting to tell a little about her experience during the Hitler period. Tante Anna was a catholic, who was a trained Froebel Nursery School Teacher. She worked for many years with Recha Loewy in Jewish Children's Homes (both in Potsdam and in Hermsdorf). When the Hermsdorf home was closed in 1935 she accompanied us and continued to look after us when we moved to the Reichenheim Orphanage in Berlin. In 1936/7 she had to leave and because she had worked in Jewish Children's Homes, she was destined for "re-education" to the National Socialist philosophy. To protect her from that, she was helped to escape to Britain, where she worked as a governess in a Jewish household. When war was imminent she felt that she had to be with her family in Germany and returned. She survived the war in Berlin and was invited by Miss Stiebel, who had been on the committee supporting the Jewish Children's Homes, to visit London. I took the opportunity to travel to London to meet her. In 1960 she visited us in Glasgow. She was a very special person.

Since we were going to Berlin we had to inform the Consul in Hannover of our journey and were given concise instructions about driving through the East German Democratic Republic. Since my passport showed that I was born in Berlin and Joe was working in the aircraft industry (Scottish Aviation) we were informed to be especially careful and not to be stopped for even minor offences, e.g. driving beyond the permitted speed. In fact, we were informed that should there be problems while travelling in the East German Republic we could not expect help.

We were also told not to stop at any time along the motorway, particularly not at any rest places. This caused some anxiety for us, since we had two small children, one under two years, and one four years old.

We were also informed to send a postcard to the consul when we were ready to leave West Germany to travel through the East German area. Also when we arrived and left Berlin. We were careful to carry out the instructions and the 100Km journey to Berlin took longer than it should have, but we arrived at the checkpoint safely and had no difficulty entering Berlin. I must admit I felt very tense and was glad to arrive safely at Berlin-Tegel where Tante Anna lived. When we reached the building where she lived, she was looking out of her window, obviously watching for our arrival.

She made us most comfortable and she asked her niece Helga to come and meet us. Helga and I were the same age and I had been invited to her 10th birthday party. For some reason I was tense meeting her again and while we talked about the past, I wished that I could have asked her about her life during the war and about her life now. It is one of my failings that prevents me making meaningful contact with people, i.e. my fear of hurting and being hurt. I did try to find her on subsequent visits and while I am very sorry to have failed, this sense of being hurt and rejected, always prevented me achieving what I really wanted.

We took Tante Anna in our car to Hermsdorf and showed Joe and the children where I had lived and the school I attended. While Joe took the children up the Siegessaule in Berlin, she and I had time to talk.

On the last day she told me that when Tante Recha was to be transported to Teresienstadt in Czechoslovakia, she had given her photographs and other memorabilia from the Hermsdorf period. She felt that it was time for these memorabilia to have a safe home and asked me to look after them. I felt honoured to do so. Tante Anna was now not very well and I was sad to take leave of her. Indeed two months after we left, her sister wrote to tell me of her death. When in 2000 I too felt that it was time to find a safe home for these memorabilia, I arranged a meeting with the archivist of the new Jewish Museum in Berlin and asked her to include them in the Museum's exhibits, which she did. However, I doubt that it will mean anything to the visitors, if indeed it fits into the general pattern as outlined in the original philosophy.

## Invitation to visit Berlin in 1990

Since 1990 I have been involved in intensive search into the fate of my family. While I knew of the fate of my aunt and her children, which my mother told me of, I knew nothing of the fates of my father, brother and uncle Abraham. At the end of the war I had contacted the Red Cross, giving them as much information as I then had about my father and brother. However, the letters I received over the years from the Red Cross always stated that there was no information available. Arolson, in Germany, held data about the Holocaust, but I always felt that the claim that they had all the information could not possibly be correct.

I should also mention that by that time we had bought a Motor Caravan and that gave us greater freedom to travel and enabled us to cover many countries and areas within each. We were a little early for the official visit to Berlin and spent the time staying in a campsite in Berlin.

This site was only for Berliners since they could not travel outside of the city during the division between East and West Berlin. However, they allowed us to camp there until the official visit when we moved to a hotel. During the few days we stayed at the campsite no one spoke to us but as we were ready to move out a man asked us what we were doing in Berlin and why we were there. When I explained and he realised who we were, he asked me, "Do you really think that 6 million were killed?" I replied, "Would it be more bearable if I said that 5,999,999 were killed? We will never know the total number who were killed. It is not just the numbers but the unbelievable evil and cruelty which made this possible."

He understood and said, "You are right." Indeed, as the years went by, more and more mass graves were identified and my answer then was not out of place.

We visited Berlin in 1990 by invitation of the Berlin Senate. The Berlin Wall separating East and West Berlin had been broken and the communist regime ceased to exist. This enabled us to visit the eastern part of Berlin.

The sharp contrast between East and West Berlin was a sad reminder of the social and political divisions of the thirties. While there, we met a historian and his group of co-workers, who were delving into the history of the Jewish area in Berlin and also had a small exhibition relating to the removal of Jews to Poland or local concentration camps. I realized that some of the information was not accurate but also understood that they had limited access to more up-to-date information. We kept in touch for many years and always met when we were in Berlin. I was sad that West Berliners considered them inferior socially, economically and academically.

In my diary I wrote my impressions and feelings about the area where I had lived and now visited. "East Berlin is most depressive to live in. There are so many ruined houses, or in poor state of repair. Although there are some new houses, there is no life about them. The Reichenheimsche Waisenhaus had been bombed and there was now an empty space. The Auguststrasse was derelict and while the Ahava building was still intact, it looked slummy, and so looked my former school, plastered with graffiti. The New Synagogue, which had escaped the destruction of the Kristallnacht, had received a direct hit during the bombing raids. The façade was intact and a policeman stood guard there." I spoke to him and he was friendly and freely answered my questions. He felt that since the wall came down there was more criminality and the police did not have the power they used to have to deal with it. It almost sounded as if he wished things had not changed.

We went to a café for a light meal. There was little they had to offer except eggs; nor was the tea drinkable. We also visited the Jewish Cemetery in Weissensee. It was neglected looking and I had difficulty finding my grandparents' graves. East Berlin was a sad and neglected part of Berlin.

The week in Berlin was well organised, with visits to various places, including the memorial to German resistance to Hitler. We went by bus to the Martyn Gropius Bau—an exhibition Centre where we were welcomed and addressed by the "Buergermeisterin". In her speech she gave an overview of the city's past, present and future prospects. She recognised that one cannot forget nor forgive the past, but she hoped we would recognise that they were trying hard to build a free and tolerant Germany.

There were other visits, including the Reichstag and a trip to the Glienicke Bridge, where prisoner exchanges took place. We were taken to the comic or satirical theatre in Berlin, which performed a satirical play making fun of the life in Berlin, its politics and its leaders.

It reminded me of "Karol's Lachbuehne" in Berlin. I was too young to visit it but my mother told me about it. The performers or actors made fun of the politicians and according to my mother, their actions were the same during the war and the content was directed against the Nazis. In fact, it was frequented by them and, I suppose, provided them with light relief. The actors certainly got away with some quite outrageous statements.

A German couple invited us to their home and we were collected from the hotel. It was an interesting experience. They lived in a nice flat and made every effort to make us feel welcome. Both talked about their lives during the war. I found it interesting that they never asked me about my life in Berlin and subsequently after leaving in 1938, yet talked all the time about their suffering. I suppose it was too difficult for them and I asked relevant questions about their lives. I did feel though that they found it stressful having us and I too at times felt ill at ease.

While I appreciated their efforts to make us welcome and provide us with an opportunity not only to visit the city where I was born and lived, as well as their earnest attempts to make us feel welcome, I found it quite difficult and at the end of it felt quite drained and wept.

I knew no one in our group and had always hoped to find someone from my childhood, but this was not to be. Those who survived have moved on just as I have moved on. Those I know who have not survived I will continue to remember and mourn.

# Chapter 22

## Journey to Poland and Czechoslovakia

Following our visit to Berlin in 1990 we travelled to Poland, visiting Warsaw, Krakow, Rzeszow and Auschwitz/Birkenau concentration camp.

There was little that I could learn about my father when he was in Warsaw since I did not have the last address of his abode. I did write to him during 1938 until the war broke out but since I had lost all my papers and letters during one of my many moves to find accommodation in the 1940s, it hampered my search now.

Since the area where the Warsaw Ghetto had been has now been rebuilt, there was nothing there to learn from or about the lives of the Jews who had been confined there. However, books have been written about this evil episode and the more recent publication of photographs taken by a German Soldier (Heinrich Joetz) of the Ghetto in 1941 provides proof of the evil and suffering of the Jews there. (The book was published in Germany in 2001.)

The only evidence about that period were the ruins of the prison, which was then used as a museum. I saw an open book in a glass case. Since the names it contained were written in Gothic print, it was obviously German. I asked the guide if I could look through it as it might contain names of people I knew, perhaps even my father's. She rudely refused my request. In subsequent visits to Warsaw I went to the newer museum where artefacts of Jewish interest were exhibited. The curator there was helpful and searched the prison book for my father's name, but did not find it. I therefore assumed that he, like all the other Jews confined in the Ghetto, has departed into an obscure past; indeed, I must accept that I will probably never know where, when or how, he died.

There was a large stone memorial, one side depicting Polish resistance fighters and the other side depicting the Jews in their pitiful state. The only evidence of the Ghetto uprising was the stone memorial to its leader Mordechai Anielewicz, but it too looked sadly neglected.

We walked to the large Jewish cemetery at the end of Anielewicz Street. The older part contained large gravestones with inscriptions in High German, indicating the period when that part of Poland was under Prussian rule. I had hoped to find some trace or evidence of known names, but this too was not possible.

The caretaker looked through the available records in the cemetery office but found no trace of the names I asked for. For many years the Red Cross has had the names of my father and brother on their books, but all the letters they sent me indicate that they too were unsuccessful in tracing their fate.

We visited the large synagogue not far from the Ghetto area, which the Germans used as stables for their horses and was now again used for services for the few Jews living in that area.

As we left the synagogue a Polish man, obviously under the influence of alcohol, spat at us and said something in Polish we could not understand—perhaps just as well. We were to see plenty of graffiti on the walls stating "Death to the Jews" in Polish. We soon learned to recognize the letters and the words.

## Krakow (1990)

Since I knew that my brother and my uncle Abraham had been living in Krakow I wanted to go there and perhaps find some evidence of their stay there. My brother had written to me that Uncle Abraham, who was a Rabbi, helped him, but I did not know what happened to him. Perhaps Krakow could throw some light on the conditions pertaining at that time.

Krakow is a very interesting city with a castle (Wawel Castle) and also a University. The buildings in the city looked almost Hanseatic in type. When we visited, it was a bustling city and people seemed full of life.

Across the river was the area where the Jews lived, had their synagogues and schools. It is called Kazimierz. History tells us that King Kazimerz had invited Jews to live in that part of Krakow following their expulsion from the German lands. In its day there were seven Synagogues and religious schools and it was a thriving community.

When we visited in 1990, there were only very few Jews living there and only one Synagogue open. This was called the ReMU Synagogue. It was very small and could only seat a total of about 20 worshippers. It had recently been renovated with money sent from past members or their surviving relatives living in the U.S.A. There was also a small cemetery attached to the Synagogue and a newly built wall made with the gravestones, which the Germans had removed from the graves.

There was also a large Synagogue, which looked black and is said to have been used by the Germans as a munitions' store. It was closed.

In the centre of Kazimierz was the 15th century Synagogue, which was then a Museum. A big square leading from that Synagogue to the centre of the town contained a small park. Just at the entrance to this park was a stone monument with the inscription describing the evil act committed there by the Germans when 3,000 Jews were gunned down and killed. There was no one there to give us information. Kazimiierz looked deserted and was empty of life.

*Kazimirs: Old Stara Synagogue built around 15<sup>th</sup>/16<sup>th</sup> century, now a museum.*

*Kazimirs Square in front of the Stara Synagogue with monument to
the 3000 Jews killed there*

It was only very recently that I learned about the fate of the Jews of Krakow in general, their treatment and transfer to the ghetto in Podgorze adjacent to Kazimiers and the final destination and death in Belzec.

Since there is no evidence or records of my uncle's whereabouts, I must assume that he shared the fate of all the other Jews then living in Krakow and were sent to the ghetto in Podgorze. While I have no evidence that he was treated differently from the others, there had been many reports that the Germans singled out Rabbis for special humiliation in front of their fellow Jews before being killed. (This fitted in well with the treatment of Rabbis during the Kristallnacht in November 1938.) However, my brother was sent to Rzeszow to a labour camp.

(Ref. *The Rabka Four: A Warning from History* © 2011 by Robin O'Neil.)

## Visit to Rzeszow and Oswiszim (Auschwitz)

Since my brother sent the Red Cross letter from Rzeszow, we decided to go there first before visiting Auschwitz.

We stayed in a hotel and visited the city. While some hotel members spoke a little English, it was difficult to communicate with people outside the hotel. This hampered our main aim to get information about the events during the 1940s.

Rzeszow is a large city east of Krakow. The buildings bore a strong resemblance to types built during the Soviet occupation. The only site we visited was an old Jewish cemetery. Since it was locked we rang the bell of one of the cottages to indicate by sign language that we wished to enter the cemetery. The lady pointed to the last house in the row. We went there and again using sign language indicated that we wished to view the cemetery. She had the key to the gate and obviously acted as keeper. She took us into the cemetery and since it was virtually devoid of gravestones, we indicated that we were puzzled. She shrugged her shoulders and pointing said, "Kaput!" When I asked whether Soviets or Germans, she indicated that the Germans had destroyed the cemetery. There was a new little shrine, which was built by survivors now living in the U.S.A.

We returned to the campsite just outside Krakow and since it was on the road leading to Oswiszim (Auschwitz), we drove towards that town and the concentration camp, which was well signposted.

My first impression, as written in my diary following this first visit, contained the following:

"When we arrived, the impression gained was that it was a 'commercial undertaking' and I thought that it was wrong." Indeed I did not realise that the original buildings had been Polish Army Barracks; however, as we went into these buildings, the exhibits and some of the signs indicated that the Germans had made good use of these barracks as prisons and later also for executions. However, these barracks were primarily used for administrative purposes. I found it strange at the time that each of these barracks was labelled as Polish, French, Italian, etc., giving the impression that they were not Jews. There were plenty of exhibits highlighting the enormity of the evil perpetrated by the Germans, e.g. the collection of cases, with the former owners' names still on them, shoes, crutches, artificial limbs, amongst other personal belongings. These were harrowing reminders of the senseless, evil actions committed by the Germans.

There was a building one could name as the Jewish building, which was opened by Chaim Herzog when he visited as President of Israel. It contained a record of the historical events of Hitler's rise to power and many of the events which occurred in Germany, which finally led to the massive incarceration of Jews and the murder of many.

There were also video presentations and what surprised me was the list of names of Jewish men who were tried and sentenced to various terms of imprisonment in 1935. This, as I have already mentioned, followed the passing of the Nurnberg Laws. Among the names was that of my father. I remembered seeing that list on the "Litfasssauele" (advertising column) in Berlin and also being told never to talk about it. I took a photograph of it since I consider it an important part of my life.

*List of names of Jewish men sentenced to prison terms in 1935/36*

During subsequent visits I noticed that this building was rarely visited by groups led by Guides.

Before we moved to the Birkenau part of the massive camp we had a meal at the restaurant adjacent to the visitors' entrance. After seeing the exhibits this seemed almost unreal.

While the former section of the camp was painful, it was still intact and served both as an administrative building as well as a Museum. Birkenau, however, was virtually a vast empty space now with only two or three barracks to be viewed by the visitors. To me, it was more poignant than the former army camp with its solid buildings and which, in some way, despite the dreadful exhibits, failed to convey to me the suffering of the prisoners and those condemned to die.

The two barracks, and most visited, on that day, was an example of washing facilities used at that time and toilet facilities with total lack of privacy, which indicated the abject contempt the Nazis had for these unfortunate human beings.

The other barrack was a replica of the type of sleeping arrangements for a great number of prisoners who had to share such limited space. It was almost incomprehensible that human beings could be subjected to such inhumane treatment. It was only when reading the testimonies of surviving prisoners that the full impact could be felt.

At that time we saw Japanese visitors coming out of the barracks, talking very animatedly. While I could not understand what they were saying, I could not help wondering how much they knew of the cruelties perpetrated by their soldiers on allied prisoners of war during the Second World War.

Beyond the railway line, where the human cargo was deposited, both dead and alive, was one other barrack still standing. There were no visitors going to it and since the door was open, we went in. There was a sign in front of it giving information so I knew what this barrack was used for. It was one of the remaining barracks which had housed the children, both Jewish and Romanies.

We entered and saw lovely murals. Near the entrance was a painting of a colourful rainbow and written above it were the words in perfect German: *"MORGEN WIRD ES BESSER"* ("It will be better tomorrow"). The one on the large side wall was a large painting of a field with cows. Unfortunately some people had defaced these murals with graffiti, which upset me very much. The sleeping arrangements were much the same as for the adults, but there was also a small room near the entrance, which may have been used by an adult. It was a painful sight and I could scarcely conceal my sorrow and anger. What made it even worse, was the presence of the ruins of the gas chambers, almost adjacent to the barracks, where these poor children were killed.

I often wondered who the artist was and found the answer many years later in Glasgow. There was an exhibition of the art works of Mrs Marianne Grant. I knew she had been an inmate in Auschwitz/Birkenau and a book was published containing some of her works, which did not contain those drawings. Neither were these exhibited on the walls. I asked her if she knew who painted the murals in the children's barracks and she replied, "I did, are they still there?" I had to tell her that sadly vandals had been active there but despite that the artwork was still recognisable. However, during a subsequent visit I saw that plastic covers had been placed over the paintings and I hope no further damage is done to them.

I recorded in my diary not only my feelings and impressions that the place had on me, but also my observations of those visiting. I was impressed by their silence and felt that they too were overcome by the horror displayed there. The young people showed interest and talked quietly and one young boy seemed quite overcome. I am well aware that not only Jews were suffering and killed, but it is important to remember that the prime purpose for the camps and ghettoes was the extermination of the Jews and that their numbers far exceeded those others who were tortured and killed.

I had not found any answer to my personal quest in search of evidence of the fates of my father, brother and uncle. I knew I had to continue my search.

Our final destination in 1990 during this journey was the Ghetto established in the town of Terezin in Czechoslovakia. However, before we went there we visited Prag and particularly the old Jewish area.

The old city, where many Jews had lived, contained Synagogues dating from the 13th and 14th centuries, but only one was evidently still in use on Shabbat. All the others were museums or contained some exhibits. In one, the walls were covered with names of Czech Jews killed during the Holocaust.

In the oldest, called the ALT-NEUE Synagogue, we saw exhibited drawings and paintings done by Jewish children while in the Ghetto in Terezin/Theresenstadt.

As in Poland, here too the official designation of the victims were either as being Polish or Czech, but not as Jews. I felt that to be wrong and still do. There has been and still is a tendency, whenever the subject of the Holocaust comes up, for people to express resentment if not irritation that we Jews emphasise that the Jews were the primary target for destruction.

As the years went by I extended my search into the roles of the concentration camps. It became obvious that they differed widely. Some were holding camps with forced labour facilities. The prisoners were worked to death; others were a combination of forced labour and extermination, whilst some were purely extermination camps.

In fact, Ghettoes existed long before and have been a fact of life for Jews since the Middle Ages. It is not surprising that the Germans used that system to herd as many Jews as possible into relatively small areas where they could control and use them and finally eliminate them.

It should also be recognised that the ghettoes too served various functions. While initially they were holding centres, with some forced labour facilities, they also were areas where people were killed or many died from starvation. The killings in the ghettoes were mainly by shootings or people were transported to their deaths to the nearest concentration/ extermination camps or killed in forests and buried in mass graves.

Another role and function of Ghettoes was the way the Germans manipulated the Jews. They gave them, on the face of it, a degree of organisational responsibility while at the same time exerting control and manipulated every aspect of life. It can be described like a "puppet on a string". Reading the stories about life in the ghettoes, the power structure within and the problems these created, it is clear that there must have been tremendous stresses and strains. Some of the Jewish leaders who were in control had great difficulties and, according to the accounts, some behaved in a dictatorial manner.

There were many such ghettoes and the most discussed were the Warsaw Ghetto, the Lodz Ghetto, Lublin Ghetto and the Terezin Ghetto. Having read about the Terezin Ghetto I felt I had to visit the area and find out as much as possible about its role in the scheme of things.

We travelled to Terezin on the 20th July 1990 and the first impression of the town itself was as an unimpressive, sleepy little town.

We made our way to the main barracks adjacent to the old Fort which was built during the Austro-Hungarian period in the late 19th century.

The office of the archivist was in the main building and, as had been my practice, I visited that office first. I have always found the archivists helpful and very willing to answer questions, as well as providing any material which might be helpful.

I was looking for names of people who had been transported from Berlin or were believed to have been transported from Berlin to Terezin. I found Recha Loewy's name and the date of the transport she arrived at the Ghetto. I was also looking for the names of my brother-in- law Henry's parents. He had been told that his parents had been sent there, but I did not find their names. In fact, they had been sent to the Lodz Ghetto and were then transported to Auschwitz. It must be said that this misinformation was very common and many of the Kindertransport children did not know where their parents and other family members were sent to and killed.

I had already mentioned this aspect in my mother's narrative.

Recha Loewy was already quite old and when she died, was cremated. When I asked how the ashes were dealt with, the archivist replied that they were emptied into the river, which ran through the town. Watching an angler there I wondered if he was aware of this fact. I know how I felt!! Anna Lohner told me that Recha Loewy was so distressed that she would not eat. I wonder if she really knew that food was not readily available and many died of starvation.

At the entrance to the barracks were well tended graves covered with roses. There were no names. There were also large stone urns. When I asked the Archivist about these she said the tended graves were Russian soldiers who died as a result of typhoid, while the stone urns contained Jews who died or were killed.

The barracks contained the usual exhibitions (Russian style) and indeed we were shown a typical Soviet propaganda film. It was the usual glorification of the Soviet army and the communist system. I left halfway through it.

A little outside of the town were the crematoria. A guide explained how many were killed in each of the ovens based on careful calculations of the capacity of each oven. I saw a room at the side of the ovens and thought that it was unusual. It looked like an operating theatre. The guide explained that this room was used for post-mortem examinations. I then noticed the jars containing organs and asked for more information. I was told that the Jews in Terezin attempted to create "relative normality," i.e. doctors cared for the sick, and those who died they did post-mortem examinations to determine cause of death.

On a subsequent visit we visited the Museum containing pictures of children's drawings, in fact the same ones we saw in Prag, except many more. It also provided a glimpse into the life of the Ghetto where the Jews created an environment in which they were able to utilise their intellectual, artistic, educational, creative and humane gifts.

It was only when I read the History of this unusual Ghetto/Camp that I really understood what these people had achieved under very difficult circumstances, attempting to create some semblance of normality.

The Germans used this Ghetto/camp as a showcase and were able to hoodwink visiting organisations like the Red Cross. An example of this was the visit by the Danish Red Cross, which was asked by King Christian of Denmark to visit Danish elderly Jews who were transported to the Ghetto. Their report to the King was that they were well cared for. (Cousin Jetty who was saved by the Danes gave me that information. She and all the able-bodied Jews were taken to Sweden in small boats by the Danish underground movement.)

The return journey took us to Nuernberg. We had been there some time before and were very impressed by the reconstruction of the damaged areas. We camped near the big stadium where Hitler used to hold his big rallies. This time there was a POP concert which was very noisy. That night I had a nightmare which included much noise and the sound of trains moving. I woke up in terror. There were no railway lines or stations nearby.

It may appear that our holidays during the 1990s were primarily to find answers, but that would give a wrong impression.

We also travelled to China in 1990 with a group from Britain. This was after the Tianaman Square protest and I thought it would be interesting to get the feel of that event and the effect it had on Chinese people.

We stayed in a modern hotel in Beijing. The room was tastefully furnished and comfortable, clean and the service was good. The staff were friendly and approachable but there was also an atmosphere of fear. A waitress I spoke to told me that she was a university graduate in Hotel management and tourism. While one could perhaps assume that her role as waitress is an extension of that course, she assured me that she, like all workers, were directed where to work irrespective of the qualifications obtained. Indeed she was carefully observed by her superiors and conversation with foreign guests appeared to be discouraged.

We were taken to interesting historical sites and our guides all spoke good English. I did manage to speak to one guide about the protest movement and at first my question was ignored, but the guide came back and said, "You saw it on TV, but I was there. We may have failed this time but will succeed next time." As an observant and, one could say, experienced individual in political dialogue, I understood his frustration but also knew that I had to be careful not to endanger his position and life.

We could choose where else to go and we decided to go to Chengdu in the north, which used to be the summer residence of the ruling family. While the Hotel was modern it was restrictive in some ways. For example, electricity seemed to be restricted and there was limited light in the evening. During the day we saw many Chinese people searching for coal in the coal slags. I also found it very sad that we saw no children on the streets. I was aware of the restrictions on the number of pregnancies allowed, but I saw no mothers with young children on the streets. Older children would no doubt have been at school. We visited monasteries, some of them very big wooden buildings. They must have used many big trees and it was sad to see extensive land erosion in many areas. No effort had been made to replace the trees used for building purposes.

We visited the "Forbidden City" in Beijing and it was interesting to see the local social organisation with their own little dispensary, run by a "Doktore" I was told. When I asked how long the training was for this role, the reply was "Six Months". We also visited a Kindergarten (nursery) and it seemed like those in other countries. The little children were well dressed and performed their little songs well. It was difficult to determine on such a visit the ratio of boys to girls. Since the number of pregnancies was dictated by the state, we were led to understand that boys were preferred to girls by the parents, particularly in rural areas, where boys are considered more valuable or necessary for work on the farms.

The Beijing Day was most interesting with visits to the Temple of Heaven and echoing phenomenon of echoing when standing in different parts of the circle. We visited a Jade factory and saw the skilful way the figurines were created.

Watching an opera was also included in the itinerary, interesting as an experience but not necessarily to my liking.

It was a most interesting and worthwhile tour and though we only saw a fraction of this vast country and were therefore limited to see life as it really is, it gave us at least a little glimpse of life there.

# Chapter 23

## Post-Retirement Activity

Retirement did not mean being suddenly without some interest or without contact with the world around us. Joe was active in the Glasgow Branch of the Royal Aeronautical Society, at times as treasurer or Chairman. He also joined the Scottish Jewish Archives Centre where he also acted as treasurer and certainly was most supportive when I was working there.

As for myself I was a member of the Yorkhill Nurses League and in 1990 became the Hon. Secretary, which I still fulfil in 2014. This aspect of my activity would cover another book showing the achievement of the League and my input. Apart from maintaining the register, dealing with correspondence and helping with the programmes for our annual Reunions, as well as writing the Leagues' Journal, it certainly kept me busy and still does.

In 1988 I joined the Scottish Jewish Archives, at first as a member, but gradually working once a week in the office and doing cataloguing, dealing with inquiries and helping researchers finding material for their Theses or 'Dissertations'. As a member of the Centre I helped to make the office/s more professional. The main purpose of the Archives was primarily to collect and catalogue the material given to us, but we also had a small library. However, it seemed that members of the Jewish community were primarily interested in their families' histories and genealogical searches were an important part of the work of the Archives.

My own interest was in the history of the Jewish people and how it impinged on the lives of the people living in Scotland. I was also interested in the early history of Jews in Scotland but unfortunately there was little or no information available, nor was there much interest in that aspect of history, which only looked at the history of the Jews in Scotland from the 18th century onward. Students made use of the available information either for dissertations or for theses, and my role was to find suitable material and, where possible, to discuss with them historical events affecting the Jews in Scotland. However, I often felt that looking only at such a limited period and also very local population failed to provide an accurate or clearer picture how Jews adapted to life in Scotland and adopted many of its customs.

Our displays portrayed different aspects of the life of Jews in Scotland and since we had also many non-Jewish visitors it provided a focus for questions from the visitors; these encouraged people to ask questions and seek some understanding of who we are and the contribution we made to the society we lived in.

A short film was made using the theme "Growing up in Scotland", which attempted to show aspects of life such as education, identifying with customs, such as wearing the kilt and taking part in National Historical events such as "Burns' Night", but it failed to explain why and how Jews developed an affinity with Scotland. The emphasis was on Jewish religious practices but failed to give clarity as to how these fitted in with life in Scotland or indeed anywhere else. There were also conflicting statements by those taking part, in their daily contacts with non-Jewish Scottish people.

As a more recent newcomer to Scotland I still have great difficulty in claiming that I am Scottish. The very fact that being asked where I come from immediately puts a barrier between the questioner and myself. While the Archives was primarily for collecting, cataloguing and acting in an advisory capacity, it also had the capacity to act as a study centre and many students found valuable information for their study.

No organisation stands still. Younger people joined the Centre and the changes, though necessary, did not fit into my perceived role or my interests, and I decided to resign from that role in 2009.

## Association of Jewish Refugees and Scottish Reunion of Kinder (SAROK)

Throughout the years I had little contact with other refugees, but this was to change. In 1989 an advertisement appeared in the *Jewish Echo* asking for former children who came as refugees to Britain in1938/1939 to join a group of ex-Kinder (Children) who were forming the nucleus of the "Kindertransport" in London. Bertha Leverton was the originator of this idea and she wanted to celebrate the 50th anniversary of her arrival in this country and to say "thank you" to the people of Britain. She successfully advertised throughout the world and got a very good response to her appeal when over 1,000 replied and attended the first Reunion. I did not attend.

She also published a book called *I Came Alone* which contained the stories from many of the "Children" telling of their experiences. Indeed, there was an increased interest generally about the rescue of about 9,500 children from Germany, Austria, Czechoslovakia and Poland which led to films, e.g. "Into the Arms of Strangers" and many books being written by researchers.

Many of the ex-children from Scotland also attended the first Reunion.

The Group in England formed their own "Kindertransport" (KT) group which then amalgamated with the main Association of Jewish Refugee Group (AJR) which was formed already in 1941, but was not active in Scotland until the year 2000.

Following the Reunion in London, we had our own version of the "Kindertransport" Reunion. The driving force was Dorrith Sim who advertised in the *Jewish Echo* asking those of us living in Scotland or those who had come to Scotland originally, but now lived elsewhere, to join a Scottish version of the Reunion. About 70 responded and attended the event which was held in Eastwood House in Giffnock, East Renfrewshire. Members had contributed memorabilia showing their arrival in Britain and photographs relevant to their stories.

We held a short, but touching, memorial service and then had a well catered meal. Despite the long period since many of the ex-Kinder met, it was interesting how many former child refugees were able to reconnect. It was a successful Reunion and we decided to continue as a group, at least those of us who still lived in Scotland as well as those who now lived in England.

Following the Reunion we continued to meet, usually in Dorrith's home and eventually decided to form a group calling ourselves "Scottish Annual Reunion of Kinder" (S.A.R.O.K.). Dorrith was the Leader of the group and she carried the burden of its management, acting as treasurer and secretary as well. She also wrote the Newsletter, keeping us informed of news from London and also of any new contacts and events further afield. Indeed, she had written stories for children, which were broadcast on the BBC Children's Hour.

The ad hoc group offered to help and since we had a professional caterer (Henry Wuga), who very ably catered for our meetings or get-togethers, we became quite a close group.

Since we were the only refugee group in Scotland we also welcomed survivors from the concentration camps who otherwise tended to be isolated. We also welcomed second and third generation family members.

Dorrith began to feel the strain of running the group and I offered to help her by taking on some of her work. When she handed everything over to me I realised that she was really ill and needed treatment. I was in a quandary and at our next meeting explained to the members the situation and asked whether they wished to continue as a group and, if so, who they wanted to manage the affairs of the group. The majority wanted to continue and I was asked to take over Dorrith's role until she was able to function again as founder and organiser of the group. I accepted.

While the basic programme did not change we now invited speakers with different roles in life. I was aware of the diverse composition of our group, particularly regarding religious affiliation; however, the majority were Jewish. I felt that it was important that we should know more of the community we were part of. We began to invite speakers from various groups active in the community such as the Scottish Jewish Archives, Representative Council and the work of the Scottish Council of Jewish Communities, which covers those who live outwith the major Jewish communities. Our own members also made valuable contributions in sharing their work experiences or special interests. We tended to be insular and members who lived further afield rarely came to the Reunions. Our funds were very limited and this too affected our ability to expand our activities to other geographical areas within Scotland.

Some of us were active in the Holocaust Education Programme when we were invited to speak about our experiences during the Nazi period to schoolchildren, adult groups, such as Church members, social groups and interfaith groups. I took a very active part in talking to many groups of children starting with primary 7 schoolchildren and, as the years passed, discussing the political and social changes of that period with senior pupils, students and adult groups.

I often felt that primary 7 children were too young to be burdened with the problems and difficulties we experienced or that they were too young to understand the enormity of events and their eventual consequences. Indeed I never spoke about the death camps or the horrors perpetrated by the Nazis to either primary or secondary schoolchildren.

It was only in later years that I would discuss my findings in my search for answers with adult groups. While most, if not all of these talks dealt with events in Germany and Poland, I never discussed my life as a refugee in this country, nor was it ever asked for by people. We should be thankful that our lives were saved and we should be thankful for the generosity of those giving us shelter.

I am fully aware of the difficulties inherent in organising, implementing and controlling the transport of the great number of children, and the even more difficult task of ensuring that each child is placed in a suitable and safe foster home. It was an impossible task, but I believe that mistakes were made and perhaps one could learn from them. Although the records indicate that the placements were to be vetted before placement and that there would be visits to the placements to ensure that the children were well looked after, I personally was not aware that this happened. I do not remember being visited or asked how I was getting on, but do remember requiring treatment for "Flea" bites. I was moved from a caring family.

Some of the problems found affected older children who had difficulties adjusting and some were even expelled from their new homes.

(Ref. *And the Policeman smiled*: *10,000 children Escape from Nazi Europe* by Barry Turner 1990. © CBF & WJR, Barry Turner.)

Many of the problems were related to the inability of the then existing social services coping with the influx of so many children and the impossibility or lack of experience by workers in that field to identify problems and try to solve them. There was the added difficulty finding placement for children of orthodox orientation or the sponsorship system where the children's parents in Germany and Austria agreed to accept the offers of the sponsors. This meant that Jewish children were placed with non-Jewish families and in some cases created difficulties for both the children and the families. There were successful integrations but also some who were not able to adjust. When the war broke out many refugee children were also evacuated and this led to another break in relationships, which had just been cemented. The refugee children had to manage, adapt and integrate, and they did, despite the problems many had to overcome. When war broke out and many adult refugees were interned, this also included some of the "Kindertransportees" who were old enough by then. Indeed, the internment of Jewish refugees, their ability to adapt and create relative normality within an abnormal situation, is worthy of a study in itself. It is also important to mention that many of us when old enough joined the forces or were active in work essential for the war effort.

We took part in oral history projects and today, books are written by former children and others. Some are made into plays and the public is perhaps more aware of the events of that period. I tend to be critical of many of the books and the interpretations given by those who experienced it, as well as those who interpret the written material. The majority of children did not understand the events of the time, nor did they have the knowledge pertaining to the history of the Jews.

Now that the Scottish Jewish Archives is embarking on an enlarged remit and will act as a Study Centre for the Holocaust era, it is hoped that it takes the opportunity to look at the historical root cause(s) of the hatred for the Jews which led to this atrocity. It is not enough to examine the oral history of those who lived through that period, particularly those of us who were too young to understand.

## The End of SAROK

In 2001 we received an invitation from Jewish Care (Scotland) that they and the Association of Jewish Refugees (AJR) London, would like to bring together Jews who came as refugees. They also stated that AJR and Jewish Care (London) provided services and gatherings and they too wished to provide these in Scotland. We accepted the invitation to hear about their proposals, but were concerned at the negative attitude towards SAROK.

As the spokesperson for SAROK I objected to their lack of recognition of the work we had been doing, despite the lack of funds. The AJR representative also accused Jewish Care for not doing enough for the refugees. I found this unfair and lacking in understanding of the situation in Scotland and told them so in no uncertain terms. I also reminded the AJR representative that we in Scotland were totally ignored by AJR despite the fact that many of us were members of AJR.

Following that meeting AJR arranged to meet me to discuss how we could work together. The Kindertransport group in London had already affiliated and retained an element of separate identity, which I felt we could also obtain. This was not acceptable to AJR and there was a rift between them and us. Indeed I received an official admonishment and told not to have any contact with their representative.

We discussed the issues at our next meeting and while there were voices who wanted to allow greater access for AJR, and indeed they felt that there was no need to have a separate group, the majority wanted to continue as a separate group.

Pressure from without was difficult to withstand, but as the pressure from within increased I decided to put the matter to a second vote in May 2007 when the majority decided to join AJR. We held a final meeting in November 2007 when SAROK ceased to exist.

I felt that we should not just disappear without any trace and decided to write a short history of SAROK. I included a short account of who we were and why we came to Britain. It was also important that there should be a recognition of Scotland's role in the care of child refugees and, most importantly, our contribution to the life in Scotland. We existed for only a short time and there were not many of us, but despite that, we did leave our mark in many different ways.

I resented the very arbitrary way we were treated and although I was a member of AJR since 1990, I did not attend meetings organised by the newly formed AJR group. It took a number of years, when the AJR representative moved to other AJR groups, that I eventually took part at their meetings, but have no special role within it. I must admit that while I felt hurt at the way I was treated, I also recognised that with the changes within AJR and, in particular, its economic and social role, it was a change for the better and I made my peace with them. We certainly could not have competed with them.

# Chapter 24

## The End of my Search for Answers

In one of the letters from my brother, sent through the German Red Cross in 1942, he informed me: "I must work but do not learn anything." He also wrote that he was in contact with our mother—hence I knew she was alive in Berlin in 1942. He wished Betty and me well. It was the last information I had from him. I now know that it was his last goodbye.

Some time after the end of the war and when the Soviet Union returned many documents to the partitioned western part of Germany, these were placed in Arolsen in Germany. Only the Red Cross had access to them. I therefore applied to the Red Cross, sending them the Red Cross letter my brother sent to me in 1942. I received regular letters from them which always stated that there was no trace of both my father and my brother. I eventually asked them to return the letter to me and later was told I could claim it from Berlin. I did so. The date was important—27th July 1942. In the Red Cross letter he wrote where he was, i.e. "in Rszezow." He was telling me that he was doing forced labour. He was by then 18 years old. I mentioned already that we visited Rszezow earlier, but since we could not speak either Polish or Russian, could not communicate with anyone to get information about the labour camp.

We decided to go back to Poland and again visited Auschwitz. There I found a booklet called *Belzec*. It took some time before I read the booklet; however, I had read a letter in the *Jewish Chronicle* written by Robin O'Neil, a researcher, about excavations in Belzec and that an estimated 600,000 bodies were buried there.

In 2002 we went back to Poland and after visiting Auschwitz again went to Krakow, where I spoke to a man in a bookshop. By that time life was returning in the former Jewish part of Krakow. He seemed to know about the fate of the people from that area. When I asked him what happened to the Jews living or working in or near Rszezow, a town east of Krakow, he, without hesitation, said that they all were sent to "Belzec". Since my brother sent the letter from Rzsezow, it seemed obvious that he was sent to Belzec.

Belzec was the first of three extermination camps. No records were kept; people arrived, and those still alive, were immediately sent to the gas chambers. However, some men were used as slave labour, as the writer of the booklet was. At that time Zyklon gas had not been manufactured and carbon monoxide took longer for people to die.

I asked the shopkeeper where Belzec was and he said about 10-15 kilometres from Krakow.

We visited the village of Belzec the next day. It is a small village with one main street and smaller side streets, surrounded by forests, about 15km from the Ukrainian border. It has railway lines running through it and a train station.

The camp is shown on the map as a memorial site, but despite many hours searching for it, we could not find it. We asked the local people where the camp was and they pointed towards the main road and also mentioned the distance. Unfortunately, we could not understand them but travelled along the road they pointed to. We travelled as far as the Ukrainian border but saw no sign of the camp.

It was getting dark and we were tired, so decided to leave Belzec. I was disappointed and felt that I really must find the camp area. We spent the night at a petrol station nearby, which also had rooms available. Before settling down for the night, I decided to visit the petrol station's shop. The manager asked if he could help me—he spoke a little German. When I explained that we had failed to find the camp, he assured me that the camp was there and suggested that if we still had difficulty in finding it, to contact him, and he would send his daughter to show us. In fact, he gave me his daughter's telephone number.

The next day we set off back to the Belzec village and again had difficulty finding it. Eventually we saw two policemen standing at a siding and went to speak to them. One of them could speak a little English and he told us that where he stood was the entrance to the camp. The sign indicating that this was a memorial site was hidden by trees and very rusty. I was very angry and said to him that this was wrong, since it was marked on the map as a memorial site and yet there was no clear indication at the site. He graciously allowed us to park there, which we would have done anyway.

I have seen many camps. Many of them are well maintained as memorial sites and the Polish Government, no doubt, makes quite a lot of money from the many tourists and others visiting the sites. Belzec, however, was in a different category. It was close to the Ukrainian border; few, if any, seem to be interested in its history, and therefore it is neglected, overgrown and used by children and others for purposes which indicated contempt rather than recognition as a camp where so many men, women and children were killed.

*Belzec concentration/extermination camp. Remains of structures, but what were their purpose?*

There was a memorial, in a somewhat poor state, and someone had placed a memorial candle on the plinth. I do not know when it was erected, nor was there evidence that the site was in any way cared for; nor was there any written information about the structures we saw.

We spent some time at the site. There were some strange looking buildings but since there was no information about the site it was difficult to know what they contained or what they were used for, but there was overgrown grass and many trees.

The ground we stood on seemed almost marshy and soft and also felt gritty. I looked down and saw what looked like shards of bones. I said to Joe, "What on earth are we standing on?" The realisation that these were possibly human bones made us shudder and with that, the horror that must have been perpetrated here became too difficult to manage. It is impossible to imagine the terror these human beings were subjected to and their suffering. All I could do was weep.

*Shards of broken pieces of bones seen at this site*

While I do not have 100% proof that my brother died there, piecing together the events and dates, it seemed most likely that once he had fulfilled his use as a slave labourer, he could not be allowed to live to tell the world what had transpired there. Belzec was only open for a short time, but within that time, it is estimated that about 600,000 people were murdered there. It must be emphasised that **the majority of those killed there were Jews.**

The story, which I read after I visited the site, is a horrendous one. The camp was destroyed by the Germans in 1943 and all those who worked there, apart from the guards, were killed. They planted trees after destroying the evidence of their criminal deeds so that the advancing Soviet forces could not be aware of what had taken place there. There was only one survivor—the writer of the little booklet. He managed to escape from the guard who was left to guard him and the metal they had collected. As it became dark, and the guard was still asleep, he ran away and a Polish woman gave him shelter and treated his wounds. He hid from the Soviets, because he was just as frightened of them as he was of the Germans, but in 1947 he emerged from hiding and told his story. This story has now been published.

I felt that my search for answers was as complete as it can be, but in 2004 the decision was made to create a memorial site at Belzec. It was primarily to commemorate all those Jews who had lived and died in the area. I do not know whether it also included those who were incarcerated in the labour camps but did not originate from the area. To commemorate the names of my father and brother, their names are engraved on my mother's gravestone.

In 2009 I received a letter from Dr Horst Helas, historian in Berlin, who informed me that a Rabbi in Berlin had been in one of the camps in Rszezow. Since I was going to Berlin to talk to students at the Jewish Museum in Berlin, I arranged to meet the Rabbi. We met at the Synagogue in the Ryke Strasse just before the beginning of the Kol Niddrei service. (This Synagogue was the only one which had not been destroyed during the Kristallnacht in November 1938 because it was within a Jewish School compound and surrounded by buildings which contained the homes of many non-Jews.)

There was just enough time to hear his story and his survival of the "Todesmarsch" from the labour camp to the concentration camp at Sachsenhausen in Oranienburg, near Berlin. It was a harrowing account. I learned that there were several labour camps there and that he did not know my brother. When I asked him what type of work they were forced to do, he said that they had to help in repairs of damaged aeroplanes. These were damaged during the German-Russian campaign. When I asked him how the selections were made to live or die, he was silent for a long time and did not, or would not, or could not speak about the selection process. All he would say was, "He was of no further use to them!" He did mention that the prisoners were not given protective clothing or masks when spraying the planes, which had been damaged during the Russian campaign and caused a great deal of damage to the health of the prisoners. He finished by saying, "I am so sorry he did not survive."

Ref: *Belzec: Stepping Stone to Genocide by Robin O'Neil* © JewishGen. Inc.2008. (Page 302 No 71 shows the date 15.8.42, when a transport left Rszezow to Belzec. Since my brother's last letter was dated 27.7.42 I must assume that he was on that transport.)

I thanked him and apologised for asking him such difficult questions. We stayed for the service and I felt utterly drained and sad.

(The congregation consisted of former Russian Jews who now form part of the Jewish community in Berlin. I found it interesting when the Rabbi said, when we finished our conversation, "I must go and get ready for the Service because the members of the congregation do not know how to prepare for the ritual of the service." Under the Communist regime in Russia, Jews were not allowed or encouraged to follow and practice their religion, so this was a learning situation for them. The service itself and the tunes sang were quite different from those I was used to.)

As far as my father is concerned, I believe that he may have died in the Treblinka extermination camp. The reason for believing that is, since he was in Warsaw when the Germans invaded and Jews were herded into the confined space of the 'Warsaw Ghetto' there, he, with millions others, would no doubt have been sent to Treblinka or other extermination camps, which was closest to Warsaw, and killed there. While there is no evidence that he perished there, it may also be that he was killed during the bombing of Warsaw following the invasion of Poland. I will never know.

In 1990 when we first went to Warsaw, we visited the site of the prison, the ruins of which was a museum. I saw a book there which was written or printed in the Gothic script. It was kept in a glass case, which contained the names of inmates. I asked the keeper for permission to peruse the book, but she refused. However, during subsequent visits, when the exhibits were transferred to another centre, I asked one of the keepers about the book and she kindly inquired on my behalf, but his name was not in it.

**Subsequent Searches**

Since 1990 when we visited Berlin on an invitation by the Berlin Senate, I felt a need to study the events in greater detail. Even prior to that I took part in studies, i.e. I agreed to answer questionnaires dealing with subjects with which I had some experience. For example, the Freie University in Berlin was doing a comparative study of education in a State School and Jewish School in Germany. Since I had experience of both types of schools, I thought that I could be of some help. Then there was an advert in the Paper published by the Association of Jewish Refugees (AJR) requesting information about life in the Scheunenviertel. Here too, although I had only limited experience there, I felt that I could contribute to that study. Dr Horst Helas subsequently published his book and it proved to be very interesting. As I have written at the very beginning about that area, I felt that since it is such a vibrant area despite its many tribulations and the poverty there, it was important that a truer picture should be portrayed than that which our fellow Jews often provided in very derogatory terms.

With the building of the Jewish Museum in Berlin, adverts appeared in the papers requesting material, which would provide a more representative picture of life of the Jews in Germany. The title of the exhibition was "Two Thousand Years of History". While I did not agree with the title, because Jews only began to form communities in Germany in the 5th/6th Century, I still felt it was a worthwhile endeavour and decided to make a contribution.

In 1966 we visited Berlin for the first time, primarily to visit Tante Anna. Just before we were due to leave she said to me, "Tante Recha had given me an album containing photographs of children in Hermsdorf. Some of these children had also been in Potsdam. She also gave me the 'Abschiedszeitung' (Farewell paper written by members of staff and older girls) which was written when Hermsdorf was due to close in 1935. It was given to Tante Recha as a farewell gesture and in appreciation of her work and care for us. I would like you to have these since I know that you will look after them."

Before her transportation to Theresienstadt, near Prague, which was a Ghetto but also contained a prison built during the Napoleonic period, she gave it to Tante Anna, since she felt that she would not survive the ordeal. Indeed Tante Anna told me that Tante Recha gave up, could not eat and died soon after her arrival there. I doubt that Tante Anna knew what went on in Terresienstadt or that the Jews there where virtually starved.

I gave Tante Anna the book *Paediatric Nursing Procedures*, which was the first nursing book I wrote in conjunction with Peggy Hunter. She also told me that my father had helped her to understand the political situation as it evolved. It also helped her to form her opposition to the Nazi regime.

Since she had worked for many years in Jewish institutions she was threatened with "re-education" to be accepted by the Nazi party. She was helped to escape to England, where she worked as a governess in a Jewish Family. When war was imminent she decided to return to Germany to be with her family.

I am sorry now that I did not ask her about her experiences during the war and how she managed to survive in Berlin. When we visited her, she also asked her niece Helga to come. (I had been invited to Helga's 10th birthday party, but otherwise had no contact with her.) Helga seemed stressed at our meeting that day and I too felt stressed and did not know how to react to her. I now feel so sorry that I did not make the effort to make contact following that visit. However, at subsequent visits to Berlin I did try to find her, but was not successful.

I was so glad that I saw Tante Anna and spent some time with her then. Tante Anna died two months later.

Now that I too am getting on in years, I have given some thought to the final destination of the material Tante Anna gave me for safe keeping and, with the opening of the Museum, I felt that here was the right place for it to be. It may not be on the level of wealthy or well-known people, but it does represent an important aspect of Jewish life, namely the care and education of young children and young people. Indeed, I would place Tante Recha in the same category of Jewish Women who were in the forefront of fighting for the emancipation and rights of Jewish Women. Jews were far advanced in the philosophy of caring and educating young children and I felt, and still feel, that this should be highlighted as part of the contribution Jews made in Germany. It was accepted and is now part of the exhibition in the lower section of the Museum. One could argue that the placement of the material is not necessarily the best, since an important item, namely the "Abschiedszeitung" from Hermsdorf, is not shown. It therefore fails to impart an important aspect that the exhibits are meant to portray.

I should also say that one of the reasons I gave it to the Museum is that I doubted that it would have any meaning to my daughters, since at that time neither had shown any great interest in that period of my life. Indeed, it became obvious to me as the years went by that they deliberately avoided any conversation about the Holocaust.

This may have been due to my mother, who often cried or got agitated whenever any programme about the Nazi period was shown and no explanation was given why she behaved like that. Perhaps we should have explained or discussed it with our children, but I personally felt that they were too young to understand at that point in their lives.

It is interesting to mention at this point that during one of our holidays, when we were near to where the Dachau Concentration camp was and I suggested we should visit it, the response, from both girls, was an almost hysterical outburst against the suggestion. I certainly felt that it was wrong to visit the camp at that point in time, but also said that as this was part of our history it could not and should not be ignored. Carole was then 10 and Marion 7 years old.

Our quest for answers to the fate of my father and brother had to wait until the girls finished their education, school and University, as well as Carole's wedding in 1983.

I retired from nursing in 1985, but after one week started as lecturer in Kilmarnock Technical College teaching students taking the Medical Receptionist Course. My mother, who was cared for in Newark Lodge, died in her 92nd year in 1988. Joe retired in 1988 and I felt that I should be with him and decided to leave the College at the end of term in 1988.

## The Scottish Jewish Archives in Glasgow

The Scottish Jewish Archives Centre was opened in 1987 and Joe and I became members. I thought it would be worthwhile to learn more about its aims and objectives and attended the AGM in 1988. Those present were all members of the committee and I was the only one from the membership. I was asked to join the committee. Though I felt out of it and unsure how I would fit in, I agreed. I had a great deal to learn before I felt able to make any contribution.

In 1990 I was asked to take on the role as Membership convener and since I had a computer (PCW) I thought I could manage.

The next year I was asked to help in the Archives Office acting as substitute to whoever was unable to come on a Friday, the only day the office was open. I agreed and was introduced to the routine of the office, which included cataloguing any material handed in and placing it in the relevant file. Obviously, a great deal of work had been done to set up the system and I easily learned how to handle the material.

It also involved dealing with any telephone enquiries as well as visitors and researchers. I could deal with most but I also realized that I required an in-depth knowledge covering the general history of the Jews and the history of the Jews in Scotland. In due course, when the permanent office person left, I took over the weekly running of the office.

Joe, who became the Treasurer to the Archives, was immensely helpful in making the room, in which the Archives was located, more workable. For example, the storage of the material was difficult to access, the boxes were heavy and I could not lift them without assistance. We were given consent to improve the situation by buying proper heavy-duty shelving. We, with some help, assembled these and also bought filing cabinets. Gradually, the office began to look more professional and more manageable.

The Archives also held Open Days on Sundays when the general public could view the exhibits collected. It was also an opportunity for them to find information about their families. Genealogy became a vital part in the work of the Archives and the Director, Harvey Caplan, specialised in that field.

We were very limited for space and eventually negotiated with the Synagogue Authority to move to larger rooms in the basement. We now had two rooms, one being the office and the other being used for displays. We also had one very successful Symposium, lasting from 10 a.m. to 4 p.m., which we helped to organise.

Time does not stand still and there was a need to bring in younger members and modernise the facilities.

Harvey Kaplan brought in younger people and they brought their ideas to bear on various aspects governing the Archives, which also included the management of the Archives. The new ideas required funding and applications were made to the Lottery Heritage Fund. We succeeded in obtaining funding which also was based on extending the role and function of the Archives. Neither Joe nor I were involved with the changes of the display room and updating the office computer and additional equipment such as a digital camera and copying equipment.

New members joined the committee.

The display room, which provided various aspects of life in Scotland such as education, politics, social institutions and photographs of Jewish personnel as soldiers, sailors and other services, became more limited in portraying aspects of Jewish life in Scotland and more like a small museum. I did not think that the time-line achieved its objectives and the wall map was not clear enough in portraying where the Jews came from. Indeed its very limitation failed to give the visitor any understanding of the historical dimension as to why Jews moved from these places.

The rich tapestry of the previous displays provided a good source for discussion and stimulated the visitors to seek information.

The use of volunteers and their role also led to friction and frustration. The emphasis was now more on genealogy rather than history.

As part of the preparation for the official opening of the Jewish Museum, Berlin Television prepared a programme and I was asked to take part in it.

An interviewer, Mrs Cissy von Westphalen, and a video crew wanted to come to Glasgow on a Friday. When I told her that Friday was not suitable, since I worked at the Archives in the morning, she asked if she could come and see the Archives and the Synagogue. I could not accede to her request without permission from the Synagogue authorities and the Archives. However, I was able to get permission provided that the interview did not take place there. They were delighted.

That Friday was a very busy day. They thought the Synagogue was lovely and showed much interest in the workings of the Archives. They took many photographs to be used for the TV programme on the day after the official opening of the Jewish Museum.

We took them home and, after a light lunch, which I had prepared before, the interview commenced. I thought the questions asked, and the professionalism shown by all, was very good. Although it was a very full day, (they did not leave until 8 p.m.), I coped well. I was promised a copy of the programme (which they kept). Subsequent to that meeting I was invited to the new Berlin Jewish Museum and took part in some of the programmes following the opening including an interview with Berlin Radio.

I continued working at the Archives until 2009, when my hearing deteriorated so that I had difficulty hearing the voices on the telephone. I had no difficulty communicating otherwise. I decided that after 22 years and with all the changes, it was time to resign. Joe had already resigned as treasurer.


**Yorkhill Nurses League**

It was also in 1990 that I became the secretary of the Yorkhill Nurses League and for the past 23 years continued in that role. During all the years I have taken an active part in its development and helped to organise the 25th anniversary of the League. This involved creating an exhibition of the work of the Royal Hospital for Sick Children in Glasgow since its opening in 1883 to the present. It was very successful and Professor Cockburn suggested that a History of the Hospital should be considered.

Miss Esther Reid had suggested that the Members of the League should also undertake an Oral History, and I took an active part in organising it. I had attended a conference at the National Library in London and was keen to help in the organisation of this project. We managed to have short training sessions with members willing to act as interviewers and managed to interview over 40 members of the League. As Secretary I transcribed many with the help of members and some paid transcribers. These are stored with the Royal College of Nursing, in Edinburgh, which was very supportive, as well as the Yorkhill Archives, which are now in the Mitchell Library, Glasgow.

We hold an annual Reunion which always has been in the form of a Study day, using themes of varying aspects of Nursing, as well as having Medical and Surgical specialists, as speakers. We started the League with 300 members but as the years passed the numbers dwindled and to date (2014) we now have only 113.

It is not only that the members are getting older, but it is also due to lack of interest of younger members of the profession and this too is due to the changes within the profession.

Ever since I became the Secretary of the League I have written the League's Journal, thus keeping a record of its activity and writing about the annual Reunions with emphasis on the programmes and the topics discussed.

It is of course a very interesting and important subject to write about, but perhaps this is not the venue to air my views and feelings. However, I have written the material for the book dealing with the history of the care of sick children in Glasgow since 1883. I received great help from the then Archivist at Yorkhill, Alma Topen, who provided me with invaluable information both textual and photographic. It is a fascinating history and is ready for completion but circumstances make it difficult to finalise it at present.

# Epilogue

Throughout my adult life I have assumed a caring role, both professionally and within the extended family. As we all got older there was a need to adjust our lives to the needs of others within the extended family. I have mentioned the care of my mother in my story, but following her death we had to give support to Joe's family, primarily those who lived in Glasgow. Syd and Kitty moved from London to Glasgow. They did not have children and as they got older required our help. Syd suffered from cancer and following a stroke died in hospital in 1989. During his illness Kitty's mental and physical state deteriorated and following his death had great difficulty adjusting.

Max, Rose's husband, had a cardiac arrest following an operation and died in 1990. We took her and Kitty with us on holiday, spending a few days in Rotterdam where we visited Larry and her family. Larry was and is a special person to whom Kitty and Syd gave great support as a teenager, and were very fond of her. It was very important that she should visit her.

The holiday was also important in that it gave me a better understanding of how Kitty coped with her day-to-day life. It was not an easy holiday. On our return Joe and I became more involved until her dementia became too difficult to manage and following assessments of her mental status and ability to cope on her own, it was decided to have her admitted to the Jewish home at Newark Lodge, Glasgow. She settled in well, but her physical and mental state continued to deteriorate and she died in 1992.

Since 1988 Joe had kept in touch with his professional organisations but this too is now virtually at an end. His memory is progressively deteriorating and our activities are therefore much curtailed.

I am still active as secretary to the Yorkhill Nurses League and we both attend events organised by the Glasgow Association of Jewish Refugees (AJR). Since I have no active role within it I tend to feel like an onlooker and not as part of a group. I have become a "recipient of care" since the role of AJR too has changed and many of the older generations are more recipients of care due to the social role of AJR and the appointment of a Social Care Person who acts as liaison person on our behalf. The emphasis is financial assistance when needed and the funds are available through Restitution paid by the German and Austrian Governments and AJR is one of the Trustees. I am impressed by the way it is administered and indeed, by the role of Mrs Myrna Bernard, the AJR Social Care Worker, covering Scotland and North England.

Throughout this personal account of my life I have tried to be as factual as possible, taking into account the events as I experienced them at different periods of my life. This does not invalidate what I have written. Others, who have lived during those periods, will tell their stories according to their experiences. Each one will interpret these differently. Historians who study written accounts of these events also give their opinions based primarily on their interpretation of available written or oral material and these may not accord with that which people, like myself, have written.

# CV

## Mrs Rosa M. Sacharin

Born in Berlin, Germany in 1925
Left Germany (1st Kinderstansport) 1st December 1938; arrived in England 2nd December 1938
Edinburgh from December 1938 – March 1941
Glasgow from March 1941 to present

Education:
Early schooling: Primary/Middle School) Postdam, Berlin-Hermsdorf and Berlin-Mitte 1931 until 1938.

From 1938 – 1941 worked as domestic in Edinburgh
Moved to Glasgow in March 1941

Re-entered education in Glasgow in May 1941
Obtained Higher leaving Certificate in June 1943

Professional Education:
1943 Sick Children's Nursing; RSCN 1946
1947 General Nursing (Adults): RGN 1949
1949 Midwifery 1st & 2nd Part: SCM 1951


Marriage: December 1959
Two daughters: 1961; 1964

Diploma in Nursing (London University) 1973
Nurse Teacher Certificate (Glasgow) 1975

Educational enhancement Extra-mural classes: Glasgow University 1962-1966
Higher Education:  BA 1975 Open University

<u>Professional Experience:</u>
Staff Nurse (Outpatient Dept. Royal Hospital for Sick Children, Glasgow) 1946
Staff Nurse (Operating Theatre – Night) Stobhill Hospital 1949
Staff Midwife – Redlands Hospital, Glasgow 1951-52
Ward Sister (Paediatric Ward) – Israel 1952-1954
Ward Sister Royal Hospital for Sick Children, Glasgow 1955-1957
Clinical Teacher – RHSC 1957-1961, 1972-1975
Nurse Teacher – RHSC 1975-1981
Senior Nurse Teacher (Paediatrics) Ayrshire & Arran College of Nursing & Midwifery – 1981-1985
(Retired from Nursing in 1985)

Post-retirement: Lecturer – Kilmarnock College 1985 – 1988

Examiner (Nursing) General Nursing Council, later National Board Scotland)
Examiner (Nursing) Northern Ireland National Board
Assessor to Northern Ireland National Board (Examinations)


<u>Publications</u>
*Paediatric NURSING procedures* – (Sacharin & Hunter) 2 Editions 1964, 1969.
*Principles of Paediatric Nursing* – Sacharin, 1980 – 2$^{nd}$ Edition 1986. 2$^{nd}$ Edition translated into Spanish and Indonesian Bahasa
Contributed to two books *Nursing Care Studies* Multiple Choice


<u>Other interests</u>
Former Member of Schools Council (Shawlands area)
Secretary Yorkhill Nurses League 1990–present (Wrote newsletters)
Scottish Jewish Archives (Committee Member, in charge of office: Cataloguing and helping researchers since 1993: retired in 2009
SAROK – Group of ex-Kindertransportees and survivors – member, and since 1996 organiser – disbanded since 2007. Newsletters and complier of Oral History of members. Written a booklet about the

group – *History of Kindertransport and Groups activities and achievements* (2008)

Talks about Kindertransport, History and experiences in Germany between the wars and the Holocaust – to Social groups (adults), Primary and Secondary Schools, University Students.

Extensive travels from 1990 to 2008 in Germany and Poland (in search of Family and greater understanding of the events/answers).

Printed in Great Britain
by Amazon.co.uk, Ltd.,
Marston Gate.